T0322797

TO SANDRA, MY VALENCIANA, WILL YOU MARRY ME?

PAELLA

The Original One-Pan Dish: Over 50 Recipes for the Spanish Classic

OMAR ALLIBHOY

photography by Facundo Bustamante
cover illlustration by Melissa Donne

quadrille

CONTENTS

INTRODUCTION

MY LOVE AFFAIR WITH PAELLA

My love for paella started at a very early age, at a small *arrocería* (paella restaurant) called Posada de San Miguel in the picturesque coastal village of Altea, in the region of Valencia. We were very lucky in that my grandparents owned an apartment in the nearby city of Benidorm, where we would spend at least a couple of holidays every year together with the entire family, nearly 20 of us. It was the most fun summer camp we could have dreamed of as children, and today still provides the most beautiful memories. Every August we would celebrate my grandad's birthday at Posada de San Miguel. This was his restaurant of choice every year and his favourite place to have his birthday paella, which quickly became a family tradition.

Since then, I would say that my relationship with paella has been eventful. I started cooking at a very young age but we never cooked paellas at home as it's not a tradition in Madrid where I grew up and – quite simply – it wasn't in my mum's repertoire. So every time we went east for the holidays, this famous dish that so many restaurants offered felt exotic and special to me. It was rare to find a restaurant that could feed a large family like ours with just one pan – a pan that would come to the centre of the table for all of us to share – and paella was the perfect solution.

It was in Posada de San Miguel that I first asked if I could go into the kitchen 'to take a look', explaining that I loved cooking and I wanted to learn. As you can imagine, not many cute seven-year-old kids ask that question in restaurants, so out of the hundreds of places I asked over the years, I can only recall a couple of occasions when I was turned down. It was my thing – I loved good food and going to restaurants was a real treat; a visit wouldn't be complete without me getting into their kitchen for a few minutes, to stand at the pass and watch, or be taught something by the burners (this was in the days before 'health and safety' fears!). It was fascinating. To this day I still remember that kitchen to perfection, with long brick-built worktops in a U-shape, the walls of the rectangular kitchen wrapped with dozens of wood fires with paellas on top of them. It had an island in the middle where they would prepare the ingredients for each of the paellas. The fire from the logs of lemon and orange trees, as well as thinner branches from pruned vines, was so fierce that the flames would wrap around each paella pan to above its rim. It was heaven, and there was so much information to process for a little kid. To this day I still dream of opening a paella restaurant.

That was my introduction to paella, but I am an inquisitive person and have since probed other people about their paella memories. Over the years, I've come to realize that anyone who has eaten a paella (as opposed to a pizza, burger, or any other dish) at least once in their life remembers it. It's quite remarkable. I think the most likely reason for this is the fond memories that often attach themselves to a paella. It certainly hasn't become Spain's national dish for no reason. For holiday-makers around the world who come to our shores and stay in the larger hotels, as well as visiting cruise liners, paella is the dish that is always served at the welcome galas and marks the beginning of their holidays. In most of these cases the paella doesn't have the most exceptional flavour, but when surrounded by tiny Spanish flags and other decorations on the grand terrace of a hotel on the east or south coast of Spain, or on the deck of a huge cruise liner on a beautifully warm night infused with the scent of jasmine and the sea, I can't think of any other dish that brings such a feel-good factor to the people eating it. It's this powerful emotional connection that I personally believe makes paella so popular and well-loved by both Spaniards and all the people we welcome into our beloved country.

VALENCIA, ALBUFERA, LA TERRETA AND THE VALENCIANOS

For those of you who haven't experienced the different regions of Spain, and to give you a sense of the place and its people, I should explain that Spain, even though a relatively small country geographically, is an immensely diverse country. The geography and climate are vastly different from one region to the next and we are made up of a concoction of different cultures and people that roamed, mainly in the last 2,000 years, through the various areas that constitute our land today. I won't go into the cultural differences in detail (that would be a book of its own), but they are many and varied, which is what makes Spain, its people and its food so rich and fascinating. This also tends to be the reason why in Spain we are often more patriotic about the region we come from than we are of our country as a whole. This has nothing to do with politics; it is purely the sense of belonging.

The region of Valencia is where paella hails from. This is a long and narrow coastal strip of land that faces east into the turquoise waters of the Mediterranean. Consequently, it is a warm, sunny place throughout the year – mild winters, hot summers, humid at times but occasionally blessed with a light sea breeze. Rain is scarce, as in most parts of Spain, which makes it an ideal place to live and sustain an enviable lifestyle. And it is not only the Valencianos who rave about it; it is a dreamland for so many, from Madrileños like me to British and German immigrants who have chosen this region to live in.

As you would expect, Valencianos love their *terreta* (their sense of belonging, culture and motherland). This *terreta* is split into three provinces, collectively called Comunidad Autónoma Valenciana. These provinces are Castellón, Valencia and Alicante. The beautiful city of Valencia itself (the third largest city in Spain after Madrid and Barcelona) sits within the province of Valencia – confusing, I know. Near the city of Valencia lies the Albufera Natural Park. It is an oasis – a fresh water lagoon fed by the rivers Turia and Júcar, surrounded by woods, wetlands and rice fields with a very rich biodiversity. This exact spot is the epicentre of paella. It is here that paella rice is grown and so where the dish has its origins.

This city of Valencia is the birthplace of my partner and her family, so for the last few years of my life I have spent a decent amount of time in and around the region, as well as gaining a deeper understanding of the Valencianos, despite having holidayed there most of my life.

It is hard to describe people of a certain place meaningfully when talking about such a broad area, but collectively I've found the Valencianos to be a giving bunch. Everything they do, they do it generously, whether in love, work, friendship, teaching or feeding (and they really know how to make a good paella!). The people I have met in the process of writing this book have welcomed me with open arms and hearts and shared their knowledge, without expecting anything in return. I felt as though I were both friend and family. You may think I am biased, but even my dear non-Spanish friend Facundo, who photographed this book, experienced this generosity first-hand and commented on it a number of times during our travels there. I do urge you to visit the region if you haven't before.

PAELLA IS A FIESTA

Across Spain, Sundays are when you gather with your loved ones. In the region of Valencia, however, this coming-together will centre around the cooking and eating of a paella. This distinction, though it may seem trivial, is important, as it becomes much more of an event. Meeting for paella means cooking it from scratch while everyone is there, as opposed to having the table set with the starters ready and the main dish in the oven, waiting for when your friends and family arrive. This is another key example of paella culture and what it exemplifies – bringing everyone together to take part in the paella preparation.

On a typical Sunday, the table might be set by one guest, while others prepare the salads, alioli and bread. Even the main event, the paella, isn't necessarily cooked by the host; it can be cooked by someone else and everyone generally helps (and messes about) with the making of it. Each person always has their own opinion on how best to make a paella, so the process always involves a lot of banter!

Meeting for paella is a whole-day event. From the aperitivo – a drink served with a few snacks – to the preparation of the ingredients and the building of the fire, to setting the table, making some starters and cooking the actual paella, the day is filled with good food and good people. And even once we've finished eating, the day doesn't stop there – in a very Spanish manner we move on to what we call the *sobremesa*, the chat and laughter that can go on for so long that, before you know it, it's dinnertime.

PAELLA FOR THE PEOPLE
- AND FOR EVERY DAY

This book is aimed at anyone who loves good food and wants to have a go at making and eating new dishes at home. In the same way that many people have a lovely curry, a warming soup, a comforting pasta, a roast dinner and a couple of decent puds in their cooking repertoire, paella should be a staple meal made week on week.

The wonderful thing about paella is that it is a complete meal – and a nutritious and balanced one at that; as the subtitle for this book says, it's a one-pot wonder! Without going full-on nutritionist about the subject, I would say that in general, depending on which flavours and ingredients you go for, a paella has the perfect balance of plenty of vegetables, a smaller amount of meat or fish and a lot of rice. All dressed with good extra virgin olive oil and, of course, the stock. It's a formula that fits perfectly under the umbrella of the famous Mediterranean diet, proven to be one that makes us live longer, healthier lives.

One of the best things about paella is that it is so simple to cook and very affordable, since the bulk of the dish consists of humble rice. Of course, making and eating a paella can be a weekend event, but it's also perfect for a midweek dinner.

Paella is a people-pleaser. Loved by everyone, it is always served with pride and joy and is welcomed at the table with immense gratitude. This may have something to do with the fact that it comes in an impressively big pan and looks delicious. But it's also because those who are about to enjoy it know how much effort has been put into making it – this is something that transforms mealtimes into something special, no matter the day of the week or who you are feeding.

CREATIVITY AND CONTROVERSY

Paella means so much to Valencianos and I can't think of any other dish in the world that is so protected by its people yet also comes with strong potential for controversy. Valencianos are always prepared to have a full-on argument, if needs be, about the difference between a paella and any other rice dish. I always find this fairly amusing (perhaps this makes it clear that I'm not a true Valenciano, only an adopted one!).

For decades, paella has been a controversial topic and an interesting talking point. Traditionalists believe that there is only one true way of making a paella with no room for experimentation, and that all other Spanish rice dishes are called *arroces*. It's an interesting debate, but I am a little less traditional and believe that, outside of Valencia, all the recipes in this book can be classed as paella if they are cooked in a paella pan. However, for the traditionalists and the curious, I have included a recipe for The Original and the Best Paella Valenciana on page 52. Truth be told, I do think Paella Valenciana is my favourite of all paellas and rice dishes. I consider myself an absolute gourmand, so that should tell you

there is something quite remarkable about this fixed recipe. Traditions are there for a reason, and if something has been loved for generations, then that says something about why it is so revered, as is the case with Paella Valenciana. Paella is only growing in popularity and expanding its frontiers, a fact that speaks for itself. Whether you are a supporter or a dissident, make sure you have fun and join in with the banter when someone brings it up.

I personally think that it is fun to experiment with food. My respected and admired *amigo* Jamie Oliver was harshly criticized over his version of a paella a few years ago and I was shocked. For me, judging someone for creating his own version of a dish is an insult, especially someone like Jamie Oliver who has shown so many millions of people all around the world how to cook and eat better. As a proud Spaniard, and as someone who dedicates my life to showing people how to cook Spanish food, I would rather see people trying to cook their own interpretation of a dish from my country, than them not trying to cook and enjoy the food of my country at all.

I love the traditional paellas, sometimes more than my own inventions, probably because I have eaten so many of them throughout my life; I have soaked in the flavours and they are ingrained in my memory. Eating a traditional paella simply makes me feel good and instantly transports me back to my childhood, surrounded by my loved ones. But that doesn't stop me from trying new things and experimenting in the kitchen.

With paella, just as with any other dish, trial and error is encouraged. Practice and experimentation are the only way you will find paella success! There aren't many crafts that we repeat daily that allow for creativity – most of us do not draw or make music daily, but we do cook daily! Trying new things in the kitchen, or new ways of cooking, is super-beneficial for your brain and belly. Feed your creativity, *amigos*!

Unconventional ingredients can lead to great results (as well as occasionally catastrophic ones...). For example, let's say you have used katsuobushi smoked tuna flakes to enrich a traditional fish stock. That would add a lot of umami layers to the stock and take it to another level. Since you've just used a Japanese ingredient, what would stop you from pursuing a Japanese-influenced paella? You could add soy sauce to your stock and infuse it with ground dried wakame seaweed or matcha powder instead of saffron, then finish off your paella by topping it with some miso aubergine and baking it for the last few minutes in the oven. The very idea of this might have paella traditionalists turning in their graves, but the possibilities are truly endless and the principles of cooking the paella remain the same, which is ultimately why I wrote this book. Whether it's a paella thrown together with whatever is left at the bottom of the fridge on a Tuesday night, or a wildly inventive and decadent paella cooked on the barbecue at the weekend, my aim is to help you master the basics of making a paella so that you can be as traditional or creative as you like. Go for it!

¡Buen provecho!

THE MASTER'S GUIDE

IN SEARCH OF PAELLA PERFECTION

Amigos, welcome to the section of the book where you will learn the art of making outstanding paellas.

I am of the opinion that cereals (by which I mean things like rice and wheat) are one of the hardest ingredients to cook with in the world. In my life as a chef I have encountered endless challenges with both, and it has taken me a long time to understand and master them. And when it comes to rice, there is no other cooking technique I find quite as challenging as cooking rice perfectly in paellas. To make consistently outstanding paellas has been a lifelong challenge for me. I have dedicated more time to the single art of understanding and cooking them than any other dish or style of cooking and I still find them equally interesting and fascinating today as I did 30 years ago.

I am one of those passionate types who thrive on investigating, learning, improving and making something better and better, which means I haven't yet stopped learning about paellas. However, I thought it was about time I put my learnings to date down on paper in the hope of helping as many people as possible discover the beauty of this dish. I hope to pass on as much digestible knowledge of this obsession of mine so that you can achieve just that.

I must confess that I have only just reached this level of mastery quite recently. Before writing this book I made a couple of trips to the region of Valencia to share and learn from some of the most talented paella chefs in the world, and this was the key to me perfecting my paellas. It was the missing piece in the puzzle; I managed to conquer more in six days than I had in three decades. As with every craft, it is only by sharing knowledge and experiences with one another that you can really make sense of your own journey. Make sure you share your own paella experiences, as it will be the only way you find other *amigos* who can share theirs with you. Don't forget to tag me on Instagram with all your creations (@omarallibhoy), so we can share and learn from each other.

Throughout my career teaching in cookery schools and in my restaurants, training both very talented chefs as well as rookies, I have come to understand how to connect meaningfully with learners and how to best pass on knowledge. I find that it's best to start by keeping things simple at every level, so I have avoided using super-technical vocabulary or scientific terms and kept things informal and light, as I would do with my *amigos*. I could easily get quite geeky about paella, but I've chosen to strip it right down to its essence so that you can master the basics and work your way up from there.

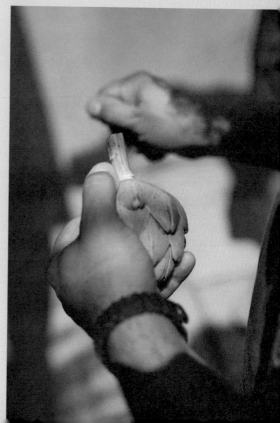

THE STAPLE INGREDIENTS

As this is a single-subject cookbook, there are a handful of ingredients that are repeated recipe after recipe. These staple ingredients are so fundamental to the dish itself they deserve to be introduced individually. The end result of your paella will be directly influenced by the quality of these ingredients, so it stands to reason that your understanding and selection of each one is essential to a happy paella.

RICE

It should be no surprise to you that paella is all about rice – after all, it is what makes up the main proportion of the dish! The rice in a paella is both the main ingredient and the flavour carrier. The rice sits centre stage, so naturally every other ingredient that follows is there to complement and elevate it.

For the purpose of cooking paella there is only one varietal of rice that lends itself perfectly to the task, and that is Japonica. It is important to differentiate it from the other varietal of rice, Indica, which is more readily available and consumed worldwide. They are very different from each other in look, taste and the way they are cooked. Popular Indica varieties are Indian basmati or Thai jasmine rice; both have long, thin grains that have a strong flavour of their own, don't absorb other flavours very well and feel fluffy in your mouth

once cooked. They are great for accompanying meals as a side dish and work well cooked simply in plain water, just as it is done all over Asia. The Japonica varietal is a shorter, more rounded grain, and needs to absorb a lot more water to be cooked to perfection. Consequently it is able to absorb flavours fantastically well, which is one of the most important aspects in making a tasty paella. The texture of the rice is also crucial to making an authentic paella. In a well-cooked paella each grain should be separate from its neighbouring grains and have a smooth mouthfeel, still with a little bite to it but not al dente or hard at the centre. With Japonica varieties we are able to achieve just that.

All along the Mediterranean coast of Spain there is a vast spectrum of Japonica rice plants growing. There are so many varieties on offer, each with their own subtle differences, that it can sometimes be overwhelming: bahía, J. Sendra, bomba, bombita, albufera, balilla x sollana... the list goes on. What matters most is they all give fantastic results to a paella. Some varieties are protected by Designation of Origin, like Arroz de Valencia, Calasparra or Arroz del Delta del Ebro. These traditional varieties are grown and harvested within a certain set of criteria, providing some of the best rice available to cook paella with. Having said that, the standards of food production in Spain are generally so high that you will find outstanding rice from smaller or larger producers too, often at half the price. Most supermarket white-label brands worldwide under the name 'paella rice' or 'Spanish paella rice' go beyond the call of duty and will deliver a fantastic paella.

My friends Edu from Molino Roca and Juan from Arroz Tartana, are revolutionizing the rice scene as a result of investigation, improvement and a relentless search for a better grain to cook paellas with (they are not interested in any other purpose for their rice). Their efforts have meant that their rice is now used in the best paella and Michelin-starred restaurants in Spain. Without going into too much detail, through the process of milling and polishing the rice, removing the husk, and discarding any damaged grains, their rice is impeccable, homogeneous and as white as it gets, with a low level of starch that allows us to create the most delicate and flavourful paellas. Unfortunately their rice is not easy to find outside of Spain, as production is limited.

After having cooked with almost every variety of Japonica rice, and because the world of rice is so vast and often confusing, I have simply referred to 'Spanish paella rice' in the recipes in this book. I will leave it up to you to discover what your local shop, deli or supermarket has on offer, as wherever you are in the world the varieties may be slightly different. As long as you're cooking with Spanish rice you will be fine. In general terms there is no better or worse Spanish rice for making paella; however, there are certain types that are better for using in dry paellas and those better for making soupy paellas – it's all about experimentation.

And to round off my introduction to rice, my one piece of advice if you are just beginning your paella journey, is to stick to one brand of rice that you can easily get from your local supermarket. This way you can learn how much water it absorbs and how it behaves and cooks on your stove, so that you can consistently produce good paellas at home. Some types of Spanish paella rice will cook in 16 minutes, others in 20 minutes, absorbing different quantities of liquid throughout the cooking process, so it's always best to get to grips with one variety or brand first. The fewer elements you change in your paella journey, the easier it will be to reliably produce great results, which is the first step to mastery.

GARLIC

Garlic is Spain's most-used vegetable – we add it to virtually everything and its scent is present across the length and 'breath' of the country. If used generously it can even lure passers-by into a restaurant. It is piquant, a touch spicy, and it imbues with flavour everything it touches. For me, the most beautiful of all its qualities is that depending on how you prepare and use it, it produces different levels of flavour: blitzed raw in a gazpacho, rubbed on some crusty bread, finely chopped and fried in a paella, sliced and sautéed with vegetables or used with the skin on to give aroma to a stew... it becomes a completely different version of itself depending on how you treat it. I can't quite think of any other vegetable that is as playful as garlic – so of course it had to be part of Spain's most famous dish.

For paella, I like to fry the garlic briefly in oil just before I add the sweet smoked paprika and tomatoes, which stops it from burning and turning bitter. Some other paella chefs prefer not to risk frying it in the oil because there is a risk of overcooking it, and instead prefer to grate it together with the tomatoes. In my opinion they are missing a trick – infusing the oil with that little bit of garlic magic will carry the flavour through until the end of the cooking process.

OIL

To me there is nothing better in the world of fats than the raw juice extracted from the first pressing of olives – what we commonly call extra virgin olive oil – and it is key to a delicious paella. Spain is the largest producer of olive oil, accounting for 50 per cent of the world's total production. It should come as no surprise then that we use it indiscriminately in all our cooking and you will never find better value olive oil than the Spanish stuff – it is pure economy of scale. So skip buying Italian brands with 'EU origin oils' and go straight to Spanish-produced olive oil. It can be found anywhere in the world these days, although depending on the country you're in it can be more expensive when compared to the local oil of that area. What's important is that you use olive oil for your paella, rather than any other vegetable or nut oil, so even if you can't get hold of the good stuff, do still use a light olive oil if that's all you can get.

The thing about olive oil is that it has a particular fruity flavour that carries through to the finished dish, and this is important to the overall flavour of the paella. In some instances, I can see why a few chefs (not home cooks, this would never happen in a Spanish home) prefer to save money and use a more affordable, lighter oil, often when cooking a meatier or more protein-heavy paella, where the fat of the meats used has rendered down and the subtle fruity flavour of the oil is no longer felt. That would be the only exception though, and I would never use any other oil than extra virgin olive oil for my vegetable and seafood paellas.

The oil has a number of duties throughout the paella cooking process:

- It fries our ingredients, caramelizing them and locking in their natural juices and flavours.

- It infuses its fruity flavour with the flavours of the other ingredients.

- It sears the rice, helping the starch to stay within each individual grain and giving it a pearly lustre and gentle sheen.

- When the stock is added, the oil will naturally float on top, providing a protective film that will act as a lid for the paella, helping to steam the exposed grains of rice once the stock has been absorbed. (This is one of the reasons why you should never stir the rice, as you will puncture the oil film and the top layer of rice will end up undercooked.)

- When the stock has reduced, some of the oil will filter through the layer of rice to reach the bottom of the paella pan again, where it will help to caramelize the layer of collagen-rich, glutinous stock to form a glorious socarrat (see page 49).

- Since oil is not absorbed by the rice, when eating your paella, the flavourful oil that coats each grain gives it a loose texture – the paella should feel very slightly oily.

SWEET SMOKED PAPRIKA (*PIMENTÓN DULCE AHUMADO*)

This is undoubtedly my favourite Spanish spice. At home I buy it in 800g (1lb 12oz) tins, which often last me about a year – I think that tells you everything you need to know about how much I love the stuff! Sweet smoked paprika is a fine powder, bright red in colour with an intensely smoky aroma. It is made by milling smoked, dried red peppers, mainly grown in the region of Extremadura. There are other paprikas produced in Spain, like the bittersweet and hot varieties, both smoked and unsmoked, but for the purpose of paella, I would like to emphasize that the sweet smoked paprika from this particular region is what delivers the best results, so

do try to get some from your local supermarket (or buy from my online deli www.thespanishchef.com).

Unlike other peppers that are dried in the sun, to make sweet smoked paprika the peppers are laid over floors made of metal mesh on the first storey of (often picturesque) smoke houses. On the ground floor a big chimney with burning oak will be fed for around 10 days, maintaining a steady sauna-like temperature in complete darkness until the peppers are completely smoke-dried. What is achieved is a bittersweet flavour, a bright red colour (as the darkness and lack of sunshine has maintained their colour) and the most fragrant and delicately smoky aroma you can imagine.

For those who haven't tried this spice before, I know it will be revolutionary. And it can be used and adapted for most cuisines – your curry will never be the same again. Like any other spice it should be lightly fried in oil for a few moments to activate its essential oils and bring its flavour and fragrance to life. A word of warning though – it is so finely ground that it will burn and turn bitter within 5 seconds if your pan is too hot. Always have your grated tomatoes prepped and to hand so they can diffuse the heat as soon as the paprika has infused with the oil. As well as the flavour it brings, sweet smoked paprika is also what gives paella its distinctive colour. When you add it to the hot oil, you will see how quickly it stains into a vibrant red.

SAFFRON

This spice is made from the dried stigmas of the beautifully purple *Crocus sativus* flower, so thin and delicate that it takes a huge amount of labour to harvest it by hand. I always find it difficult to describe the taste of saffron as there is nothing quite like it – I often end up saying the same thing, when asked: 'It tastes like saffron.' To date I haven't found another flavour that even vaguely resembles saffron, and that is what makes it so special and irreplaceable.

People often think that saffron is added to paella for the colour it provides, and can easily be replaced with orange food colouring. This really frustrates me – food colouring gives a bright, luminous, nearly fluorescent yellow that just shouts 'fake tan'! Paellas are beautiful in all their natural shades – greenish due to artichokes, brownish as a result of the caramelization, and yes, orange from the saffron and paprika... but for some strange reason the brightness of paellas has been taken out of context and become what people think of as 'paella'. Saffron is a delicate and special spice and is used primarily to impart flavour rather than colour to the dish.

Saffron is the most expensive spice in the world – and it is worth every penny. So many flowers are needed to produce just one gram of this hand-harvested spice that its high price is justifiable. Yes, the upfront cost may seem daunting, but I urge you not to be put off – you need to use such a small amount of saffron when cooking that it works out as an affordable amount per person for what is a very special ingredient. Depending on the quality you can get hold of you should use something between 0.05g to 0.1g per person. The better the quality, the less you'll need to use.

In Spain we produce a small amount of this very precious spice, yet it is of the highest quality. That is why DOP Azafrán de La Mancha is the most expensive saffron you can buy. The whole crop is sold out every year so I don't need to oversell it to you – quite the opposite. You can also purchase amazing-quality saffron grown in Iran and various other countries for a third of the price of the Spanish stuff, so do shop around. Just ensure that you are not being scammed – as with all valuable items, fraud is an issue, so be sure you are buying your saffron from a reliable source. My website is a good place to start!

Currently I buy around 6kg (13lb) of saffron every year for my restaurants, at a cost of about £30,000. Because of this, I now have a dedicated saffron dealer (yes that job does exist!) to teach me everything he knows about the subject to ensure I make the most informed decisions when choosing and buying saffron.

We've also worked on how to get the most flavour from each valuable stigma and after numerous trials this is what we have concluded:

0.1 GRAMS
(small pinch)

- Dry toast the saffron just slightly.

- Pound it with a pestle and mortar to a fine powder.

- Infuse the powder in warm water or stock for 10–20 minutes before it is added to the rice.

0.2 GRAMS
(medium pinch)

In practical terms, this means adding your saffron to the warm stock 20 minutes before you add the stock to the paella pan if you are using threads, or 10 minutes before you add the stock if you have ground it to a powder. The remaining infusion time will be covered by the cooking and resting times of the paella. This is the best way to get the most flavour from your saffron (and therefore the most value for money).

0.4 GRAMS
(large pinch)

Use this lifesize image as a guide when measuring saffron. It will be particularly helpful if you don't have a micro scale.

DRIED ÑORA PEPPERS

This sundried, round red pepper is very special, but unfortunately it is rarely found outside of Spain. It is not even widely used within Spain itself, but it has a particular flavour benefit when cooking seafood and vegetable paellas as it gives an unusual fruity and toasty flavour and aroma, which is very characteristic of this style of paella and more soupy rice dishes. It is important to fry the peppers gently to make the most of them, activating their essential oils and releasing vast amounts of fragrance, smokiness and heavily roasted coffee notes.

I give instructions on how to use them in each recipe, but generally they are gently fried, then blended with the tomato or used whole in the stock to infuse and rehydrate. If they are used whole to infuse the stock, don't actually eat them as they have a prominent bitter taste.

If you can't get hold of dried ñora peppers I have good news! You can get very similar flavours in the form of dried sweet pepper flakes, which are available from most world food stores. Simply fry the flakes with the garlic before adding the sweet smoked paprika and the tomatoes.

TOMATOES

What a tasty and velvety fruit this is – especially when ripened on the plant under a warm sun, which is something most of us can only dream of if living in colder climates. In many countries, tomatoes have to be imported from afar, refrigerated while still green and then struggle to ripen into a half-decent fruit. Tomatoes are widely consumed in Spain and those we produce are revered. We put lots of effort into choosing the perfect tomato for different purposes and our fridges at home will be stocked with lots of varieties – some for salad, others for sauces, and those for paella. For paella you ideally need tomatoes with a high content of pulp and little liquid content; in other words a 'meaty' tomato that has achieved maturity. I recommend you leave your tomatoes out of the fridge to give them a chance to develop some flavour and a softer texture. Tomatoes for paella should be grated using a coarse cheese grater, which peels them in the process, but you can blitz them too in a food processor. Of course, you can use shop-bought passata or cans of chopped tomatoes instead. In fact, depending on what time of year it is and where you live, it is often better to use canned tomatoes over out-of-season fresh tomatoes. If this is the case, just make sure you buy the best canned variety you can afford.

STOCK

One of the main ways to achieve big flavour when cooking is to use rich-tasting stocks, but this is even more crucial when the main ingredient for your dish is rice, as with paella. The stock you use will be absorbed in its entirety when cooking paella, locking in huge amounts of flavour. For the purposes of this book, I have given a few recipes for stocks that will work with all the recipes. To take your paella to the next level, turn to page 44 for more detailed information on stock, as well as the core recipes on pages 157–163.

ALIOLI

Spain's ketchup, as I call it, has a sensational flavour and is a great accompaniment to so many seafood and vegetable paellas. Some people are addicted to it and serve it indiscriminately with all their paellas. I personally prefer to save it for a good seafood paella. It is a bit like lemon; if you squeeze it over everything then you are not allowing your palate to enjoy the differentiated flavours within your dishes, so go easy with it! Find four classic recipes for homemade alioli on pages 166–167.

THE PAELLA PAN

Paella begins and ends with the pan – a wide frying pan with two handles that gives its name to what has become Spain's most famous dish. Many people will argue there is in fact no paella without the paella pan. I disagree, as the recipes themselves are so much more than the pan they are cooked in. Ultimately the pan is just a utensil – admittedly a very special one – and if you don't own one it's not the end of the world as you can simply use the widest frying pan you have at home. I have cooked frying-pan paellas dozens of times with fantastic results. I wouldn't try to make paella in a frying pan for more than two people though; if you try to squeeze in any more servings the pan simply won't be big enough.

Having said that, while I want you to cook paella regardless of the equipment you have at home, I would also strongly encourage you to buy a proper paella pan. Not only will you be able to cook outstanding paellas with it, but you will find yourself using it for other dishes all the time, as it is the ultimate ovenproof pan. I am convinced that if you go ahead and purchase one (check out my online shop) you will use it more often than most pans or oven trays you already own. I cook pizza in mine – first on the stovetop then flashed under the grill; I bake the biggest apple tartes Tatin; I cook sauces to which I add boiled pasta and then top with cheese and bake in the oven.

I sauté stir-fries and fried rice as the pan imitates a wok perfectly. I could go on and on! Return on investment is guaranteed.

You may ask yourself, why can't I cook a paella in a pot, saucepan or casserole dish? Well, paella is such a special dish that we Spaniards had to engineer a pan that allowed us to achieve the best flavour and texture possible. The reason why paella pans are so wide and shallow is to achieve the perfect cook.

Perfect paella = (rice / stock) x (heat + pan size) / time

This ratio is far more controllable on a wider, shallower surface. The more people you cook for, the wider the pan must be, not deeper as is common for most other dishes. This is why there are more sizes of paella pans in the world than any other pan, and is why you see giant paellas being cooked for celebrations in villages. A world-class paella has to have the right texture, and this texture is impossible to achieve if the depth of the rice layer is more than 2cm (¾in).

There are many different types of paella pans out there. The most traditional, widely available and affordable of them all is made of polished carbon steel (the same material used to make woks). What is special about this pan (odd as

this may sound) is that it oxidizes and reacts to certain ingredients, giving the resulting paella a slight metallic taste that is very much part of the flavour of the paella we all know and love. Over time, the pan naturally ages and improves with use, creating a patina that makes it increasingly non-stick. The only downside of this type of pan is that it requires care and maintenance. It is of utmost importance that you dry it completely after each wash then give it a light coating of oil using some kitchen paper – this will protect it until the next use.

Other types of paella pan do not need the same maintenance and come in all sorts of different materials: non-stick, cast iron, polished stainless steel, reinforced stainless steel, enamelled coated steel, enamelled coated cast iron... They are all great options and pretty much do what they say on the tin; enamelled steel is light and user-friendly (I recommend getting one of these as a beginner) and reinforced and cast-iron pans need to be allowed time to heat up. Another thing to note is that paella pans traditionally have a slightly concave surface and therefore don't sit completely flat, so you will need to purchase a flat paella pan if you're going to be using it on an electric or induction hob.

The final option, and my most-loved, is a clay pan. These are what were used to make paella many generations ago. If you subscribe to my YouTube channel, you will know that I love using a wide variety of terracotta clay pans from Spain. They connect me to the roots of my cooking culture and the recipes I treasure. However, these are the most challenging pans to use so I would only recommend cooking with a clay pan once you feel confident in your paella-making abilities.

When considering the size of pan you need, I always recommend buying the most suitable pan for your cooking apparatus. As a general guide, you want to use a pan that is 14cm (5½in) wider on each side than the outer edge of your ring burner, whether using the hob in your kitchen or a butane gas burner in your garden. For example, if your ring burner is 12cm (5in) in diameter (a very common size) then the largest paella pan you should buy is 40cm (16in) in diameter.

THE HEAT SOURCE

STOVETOP

Most of us cook on gas, electric or induction day in, day out. This is where you will likely cook most of your paellas – in the comfort of your kitchen where you have full control over the heat. You can make fantastic paellas this way and I recommend this approach when starting out on your paella journey.

RING BURNER

When making bigger paellas, or when you want to cook outside, it's common to use a large ring burner set over a tripod connected to a propane or butane gas bottle. These are fun to use but are trickier to control as they commonly have two, three or even four rings distributing heat. You'll also likely be cooking in a larger pan, with more ingredients to keep an eye on. When cooking on a ring burner remember that even when you turn off the inner ring it will continue to receive the conveying heat from the ring that is still alight, and therefore continue to cook, albeit at a slower pace.

CHARCOAL BARBECUE

I love cooking paellas on my kettle barbecue, so much so that I even installed a metal pizza ring (you can find these online) onto my barbecue. This metal ring is supposed to support a pizza stone, but instead of using the stone, I use it to balance my paella pan on. It also means

that I have easy access to the hot charcoal – whereas before I would have had to remove the pan and the grill to adjust the positioning of the charcoal, I can now simply use the opening in the middle of the pizza ring to access it.

Controlling the heat is the hardest thing about cooking paella on a barbecue so if you're going to attempt it, make sure you have easy access to the charcoal, an implement to poke and move the charcoal around, heatproof gloves and some water to hand in case you need to reduce the temperature of the coals quickly. Also do remember that you can always lift the pan off the heat and pop it on the ground for a moment if things get too hot – the worst thing you can do is let the ingredients burn.

Charcoal will give you really high heat at the beginning of your cook, when the coals are red hot, which will then die down as you continue cooking. This is not ideal, as you can easily burn your ingredients when you are caramelizing them at the beginning of the process, and then be left without enough heat to boil your stock and therefore cook the rice. I normally add a generous amount of charcoal to the centre of my barbecue (about 75 per cent of all the total charcoal I plan to use) to generate direct heat under the middle of my pan. I then add the remaining 25 per cent of charcoal about 30 minutes afterwards, directly on top of the previous lot of charcoal. This creates a lid effect, capping the fierce high heat and allowing you to have some control when you are halfway through browning your ingredients. By the time you finish your base and pour in your stock, the extra heat from the fresher charcoal kicks in, helping you boil rapidly for 10 minutes. After that time, you may need to disperse the charcoal a bit to help lower the heat. If you find the heat is still too strong, simply move all the charcoal into the edges of your barbecue in a ring, leaving the middle of the grill empty. The heat on the edges will convey into the centre of the pan and will continue to cook the paella, but at a lower temperature (this set-up is call 'indirect heat' and is a very common technique when cooking large pieces of meat low and slow on the barbecue).

WOOD FIRE

Undoubtedly, the most traditional way of cooking a paella, as well the most difficult, is over fire. Valencia is a region famous for the citrus trees and grape vines that grow everywhere and it is traditional to use the wood from the pruning of these trees and the branches of the vines (called *sarmiento*) to fuel the fire (see photo on page 40). Traditionally a metal stand sits 30cm (12in) above the ground, with a log fire below and the paella pan perched on top. This makes the fire easier to control as you have 360-degree access to it and can adjust the logs

as necessary. As with charcoal, there are similarities in the pattern of the heat, but the difference here is that you'll get much more prolonged heat from large logs. Due to this, some Valencianos prefer to create a fire pit 45 minutes ahead of cooking, to give the wood a chance to burn down a little and therefore give off a more stable source of heat. As with any wood fire, the larger the logs you use the longer and more consistent heat you are going to achieve – the thinner the branches or logs the more immediate, intense and short-lived the heat. I prefer to use larger logs for cooking the base of my paella, then add thinner branches to the fire when I pour in the stock to ensure a good 10 minutes of intense fire. I then spread out the burning wood underneath the pan to reduce the heat and slowly allow the socarrat to form. Controlling the heat can be a full-time task in itself, so make sure that you are well prepared and that you have people on hand to help manage the fire (and feed you snacks and drinks).

OVEN

There is one dish that requires a special mention, and that is the Arroz al Horno (or *Arròs al Forn* as it is written in the Valenciano dialect) on page 63. It is special because it is cooked in an oven; however, almost any paella can be cooked in the oven if needed and it is a very common technique, particularly in restaurants like mine where we don't have a burner available for 30 minutes for every single paella that is ordered. You still need to cook the base of your

paella on the stovetop, but
once that is done you can add the
rice and stock and place it in a
hot oven. There are a few things to
remember if cooking your paella this
way: you will need to use less stock
as it absorbs it at a slower pace;
and a socarrat will never form but
instead a thin crust will be created
on top, due to the dry heat of the
oven, particularly if it is fan-assisted.
The oven method comes in extremely
handy if you are cooking paella for
lots of people at home without any
specialized equipment, such as a
90cm (35in) wide paella pan, ring
burners and so on. In this case,
simply cook the base ingredients in
a big pot, divide this between a few
roasting tins along with the rice and
stock, then bake in the oven for
20 minutes on the highest heat.
You can achieve fantastic results with
this convenient method when you
are faced with such circumstances.

THE FOUR KEY ELEMENTS FOR WORLD-CLASS PAELLA

THE BASE

Firstly, when making a paella, frying the main ingredients in the correct order will help to create caramelization, which in turn will deliver the most flavour to your paella. It is simple – the more colour you achieve on your ingredients the more intensity of flavour they will have. This all happens before your wet ingredients are added, such us the grated tomato (or salmorreta – see page 164) and water or stock. The caramelization created by your main ingredients will dissolve in the liquid, creating a rich stock that will ultimately be absorbed by the rice. Therefore, it is important that you fry off the main ingredients properly. Begin by adding larger, harder or thick-cut items to the pan first, allowing them time to fry and gain colour before adding more delicate or finely sliced ingredients. Once the main ingredients have a good amount of caramelization, the garlic and paprika are added in quick succession and fried for just a few seconds to avoid them burning and turning bitter. The grated tomato (or salmorreta) is added to the pan to bring an abrupt stop to the caramelization and begin the process of deglazing the pan. Think of the tomatoes as your safety net ahead of the water/stock and rice being added.

THE STOCK

In good restaurants, food tastes substantially better, for the most part, because we use homemade stocks in our kitchens and use them in a range of dishes. I know that making stock at home is an alien concept for many home cooks – often we don't have the time to create our own stocks, and we need convenient alternatives that allow us to rustle up meals quickly. But I promise you that making your own stock is well worth the effort – your paellas will be the better for it. Cooking is like everything in life – what you get back comes down to what you've put in. The better the ingredients you put into your stock, the more distinctive and fragrant it will taste. The more generous you are with the ingredients within your stock, the richer and fuller-bodied the flavour will be. It is simple really!

When making stocks there is an optimum time for how long you should simmer your ingredients – please don't leave them simmering for hours in the mistaken belief that the stock will get more delicious. The flavours will concentrate, but the stock will also become cloudy and the flavour a little bitter. Particular attention should be paid when making delicate seafood stocks, which can easily turn bitter and

develop a urine-like aroma, which should be avoided at all costs. If you are looking to really concentrate the flavour of your stock, follow the stock recipes I've given in this book, strain them and then slowly reduce them by half over a low heat.

When you really don't have time to make stock, or don't have any in the freezer, you'll need to use shop-bought stock. I do it all the time and that's what they are there for, so there's no shame in using them. There are so many forms of ready-made stocks available (fresh, tetra-packed, powdered, bouillon, paste, cubes), from so many different brands, that sometimes it's hard to know what to use. After experimenting a lot, I've found that – as with most ingredients – the more expensive the stock, the better the quality, so try to buy the best you can afford.

And finally, a more geeky note on stocks: fundamental to paella perfection is understanding the importance of collagen. Collagen is the most abundant protein in an animal and of extreme importance for our nutrition and general health. It is the glue that keeps animal bodies (us included) together, from the tendons, organs and ligaments, to skin, hair and joints. When you simmer meat in water to create stock, the collagen is released into the water. If you reduce your stock until there is very little left, like a demi-glace, you will notice it begins to get thick and tacky. Rub some between your fingers – it should feel slightly sticky. Collagen is the reason for this. Using a collagen-rich stock in your paella ensures that every ingredient is coated in a thin film of delicious flavour as the stock is absorbed by the rice.

How much stock do I need?
This is possibly the trickiest part of cooking a paella for the first time, as it is really hard to calculate. Unfortunately the answer is rather vague as it comes down to so many factors and variables, such as heat intensity, time, quantity of rice, size of the pan, altitude (cooking at sea level is not the same as cooking in the Alps), the temperature outside, the rice varietal you are using...

As you can imagine, to master paellas, considering all the variables mentioned above, takes a decent amount of practice. In general terms, if cooking a paella on the stovetop at home, using regular supermarket Spanish paella rice, and not overfilling your paella pan, you will need about three times the amount of stock (in volume) than the weight of rice. For example, for 300g (1½ cups) rice you will use 900ml (3¾ cups) stock. The less rice you add to your paella pan, the more the liquid will be able to absorb and the more flavour the paella will have, as the stock will concentrate a lot. The higher the heat the more stock you will need. So again, in practical terms, if you cook a small amount of rice in a wide paella pan using logs and small branches that produce the highest heat imaginable, then your ratio of rice to stock may well be nine-fold, so for 300g (1½ cups) rice you may need 2.7 litres (11 cups) stock. Similarly, the opposite happens if you use a small paella pan with plenty of rice and ingredients and cook it over a small burner at home; you will be lucky if it absorbs one and a half times the stock – so for 300g (1½ cups) rice you may only need 450ml (2 cups) stock. As you can see it is not an exact science and it takes practice and mastery to calculate by eye the needs for your paella in each of the circumstances. My advice is that you make a note on page 170 of what works best for you at home and then work from there. Note down how much rice you added, how much stock, how long you cooked it over what level of heat and then write about the result, so that when you come back to cooking another paella next time, you use your notes as a guide and adjust accordingly. It may have been too wet by the end or perhaps you ran out of stock and your rice was a bit too al dente to your liking; maybe it was too salty. Whatever it is, you will find your notes incredibly useful next time around.

THE COOKING OF THE RICE

I have spoken at length about rice on page 27, but here I want to talk about the cooking process of the rice. Spanish paella rice can be cooked in two different ways, both equally traditional, yet they will deliver slightly different results, particularly in their texture.

You can either add the rice after you have finished cooking your base, frying in the oil for a couple of minutes and stirring constantly so that the oil impregnates the rice and it hardens slightly, acquiring a pearl-like look, before pouring in your stock.

This process will protect each grain of rice, keeping the grains more intact even after all the stock has been absorbed. The resulting texture will be a touch more loose and fluffy with slightly more flavour on the outside of the grain than the inside.

The other way of cooking the rice is to pour your stock into the pan after you have cooked your base, let it simmer and then add the rice to it. This is the method for the Paella Valenciana on page 52, but it can be applied to all the paellas in this book.

When cooking Spanish paella rice, it usually takes about 16–18 minutes for the stock to be gradually absorbed and to evaporate. There is a stage during the cooking process where the stock and rice level out (after approximately 10–11 minutes) and from that point onwards some of the rice is left exposed, without any liquid to absorb, as the stock level lowers. Spanish paella rice is delicate and difficult to manage, as it overcooks easily; for this reason the deeper and more narrow in width your cooking vessel (and therefore the thicker the layer of rice), the longer it would take for the stock level to reach the bottom of the pan and so the longer the top layers of the rice will be exposed. This will result in undercooked rice on the top and stodgy, overcooked rice on the bottom.

You must be thinking, why don't you simply stir it like you would do when cooking any other rice dish? If you do this, you encourage the rice to release its starch and will be left with a stodgy paella with grains of rice that clump and stick together. This is why paella pans (and the dish itself) have to be flat and thin – the thinner the layer of rice the better – and you can only achieve this with a wide, shallow pan. I know, just the thought of not stirring the rice can be daunting, but trust the method and control the heat – your patience will pay off.

For mellow and soupy rice dishes, I normally add 60–80g (2–2¾oz) of rice per person. For 'dry' paellas I normally add 90–110g (3–3¾oz) of rice per person, depending on the amount of meat, fish or vegetables that are in the dish (the more main ingredients, the less rice you add).

Troubleshooting: If you notice the stock is evaporating too fast, reduce the heat to low or even cover with a lid to allow the rice to steam. If, on the contrary, you added too much stock, the easiest thing would be to remove some of the liquid with the help of a ladle as soon as you are aware of the excess. Alternatively, keep the paella on high heat for longer than the original 10 minutes to give the stock the opportunity to evaporate at a faster rate than it would normally, but make sure you don't cook the rice for longer than it should in total. The other solution is to just embrace the soupiness of your paella!

THE SOCARRAT

Revered by most, hated by a few, the socarrat is enigmatic. When done right this thin layer of crunchy fried rice at the bottom of the paella is a delight (in my opinion), but like many things in life, achieving it is not always an easy task. A socarrat is evidence of a perfectly executed paella from beginning to end, using a rich stock, good ingredients and a little bit of what the French would call *savoir-faire*. To create a perfect socarrat (and I mean 'create' – it doesn't just happen by burning the bottom of your paella), you need to be generous with the olive oil (don't make the mistake of not using enough because it will be 'healthier'). You also need to use a stock that has formed through the slow simmering of a bounty of ingredients that means it is rich in flavour, texture and with a heavy load of binding collagen. And you need the rice to release just the right amount of starch, which you'll achieve by not stirring it – a socarrat only happens when the paella is left undisturbed to form a crust.

Troubleshooting: Having said all of that, one of the main difficulties in cooking a perfect paella is judging whether or not your socarrat has formed yet. Since the socarrat forms below the rice, you need to use non-visual tools to tell if it is done. The socarrat will talk to you as it forms, so listen carefully – when the simmering sound of the liquid stops it should be replaced by the sound of the remaining oil frying the rice at the bottom of the pan. Once this frying sounds 'crisp' your socarrat should almost be ready. And don't forget to use your sense of smell – it should smell rich and caramelzied, *not* burnt. It will take a few attempts to achieve a perfect socarrat, but there is nothing quite as satisfying as mastering it.

PAELLA VALENCIANA
(THE ORIGINAL AND THE BEST)

SERVES 5   **PREP 20 MINUTES**   **COOK 1 HOUR 10 MINUTES**

This famous Spanish dish brings friends and family together. If the weather allows (which back home happens most of the time) we cook it on an open fire. This paella recipe is very much untouchable – the Paella Valenciana is regulated under strict guidelines and the watchful eyes of most Valencianos. Only very small variations are permitted and have a stamp of approval. If you follow the recipe carefully be assured that you will enjoy the best of all paellas – I guarantee it. *¡Buen provecho!*

0.5g saffron (see page 33 for a measuring guide), ideally from La Mancha
1 tbsp rock salt, to season the pan
120ml (½ cup) Spanish olive oil
400g (14oz) chicken on the bone, cut into large pieces
400g (14oz) rabbit on the bone, cut into large pieces
6 garlic cloves, finely chopped
1 tbsp sweet paprika (unsmoked)
2 small tomatoes, grated
4 litres (16 cups) water
100g (3½oz) cooked garrafon beans
200g (7oz) runner beans, cut into 4cm (1½in) pieces (preferably ferraura or tabella varieties)
500g (2½ cups) Spanish paella rice
2 sprigs of rosemary
Salt and pepper, to taste

Wrap the saffron in foil and toast it for 30 seconds on each side in a paella pan set over a medium heat, or over an open flame. Remove from the foil and use a pestle and mortar to grind it to a powder; set aside.

Place the paella pan back over the highest heat and season around the edges of the pan with rock salt. Pour in the olive oil, add the chicken pieces skin-side down and fry for 10 minutes. Add the rabbit and continue to fry on all sides for 10 minutes, turning regularly, until dark golden. Take your time, as the flavour added to the pan here is what will season the water you add later, creating a rich stock.

Lower the heat to medium. Push the meat to the edges of the pan to free up some cooking space, letting the oil run into the middle of the pan. Add the garlic and cook for 30 seconds, then add the paprika and the grated tomatoes. Cook for 4 minutes while stirring until the tomatoes have lost most of their juice and have formed a paste that is starting to separate from the oil.

Pour in the water, sprinkle over the ground saffron, add the garrofo beans (and the snails if you are using them) and let it simmer for around 20 minutes. The caramelized bits caught on the base of the pan will dissolve to form a rich stock. Add the runner beans (and red pepper and artichokes if you are using them) and let it simmer for a further 5 minutes. Taste the liquid; the rice will absorb a lot of saltiness, so it should taste over-salted at this point.

Increase the heat to high and pour in the rice, spreading it evenly throughout the entire paella pan. Cook for 10 minutes, then reduce the heat to low and cook for 5–7 minutes, without stirring. When the liquid level has reduced to just below the rice, add the rosemary on top of the paella. Cook for a few minutes longer, then let it rest off the heat for 5 minutes before serving.

ADDITIONAL OPTIONAL INGREDIENTS OR VARIATIONS

150g (5oz) cooked snails, drained
5 baby artichokes (use canned if you can't find fresh), halved or quartered depending on size
1 red (bell) pepper, deseeded and cut into strips
Use cooked butter (lima) beans instead of garrafon beans
Use duck instead of chicken
Use pork ribs instead of rabbit
Use light chicken stock instead of water

NOTES IF YOU ARE COOKING THIS RECIPE OUTSIDE OF VALENCIA

Two fundamental things need to be considered when cooking this simple recipe outside of Valencia. The first is that it's unlikely you'll be able to find all of the ingredients – this is why I have given some alternatives. The second is that the ingredients in the region of Valencia are second to none; the year-round sunshine and rich soils deliver strong flavours that elevate our produce. If you follow this recipe exactly but use low quality ingredients, you're likely to be slightly disappointed by the end result. Your paella will probably lack flavour and richness. To solve this, I recommend using a light chicken stock in place of water, which will add richness and make up for the deficiencies of your other ingredients.

MEAT PAELLAS

ARROZ DE CARRILLERAS

BEEF CHEEK, CARROT AND CHICKPEA PAELLA

SERVES 4   **PREP 20 MINUTES**   **COOK 3½ HOURS**

Beef or pork cheeks are a sublime cut: when properly cooked they are meltingly tender. They benefit from long, slow cooking – but I promise this paella is worth the wait.

100ml (scant ½ cup) olive oil
800g (1lb 12oz) beef cheeks
3 carrots, cut into small batons
1 medium onion, chopped
1 celery stick, finely chopped
6 garlic cloves, chopped
2 tomatoes, chopped
2 bay leaves
¼ cinnamon stick
2 cloves
1 tsp sweet smoked paprika
5 black peppercorns
175ml (¾ cup) red wine
3 litres (12 cups) water
100g (½ cup) dried chickpeas
   (garbanzo beans), soaked in
   water for 24 hours
400g (2 cups) Spanish paella rice
Salt, to taste

Heat the olive oil in a wide pan over a medium heat. Season the beef cheeks with salt and pan-fry for 5 minutes on each side. Add the carrot, onion, celery and garlic and fry for 10 minutes until well browned. Add the tomatoes and reduce down for 3 minutes, stirring to deglaze the bottom of the pan.

Add the bay leaves, cinnamon stick, cloves, paprika and black peppercorns, then add the red wine and reduce for a minute. Pour in the water, reduce the heat to low and add the chickpeas. Let them simmer gently for the next 3 hours until both the chickpeas and cheeks are soft to the touch.

Add the rice and give it a good stir, distributing it evenly, then taste the liquid and adjust the seasoning if necessary. Cook over a high heat for the first 10 minutes, then reduce to medium and cook for another 9 minutes, without stirring. Let it rest off the heat for 5 minutes before eating.

ARROZ DE MATANZA

PORK FEAST PAELLA

SERVES 4   **PREP 30 MINUTES**   **COOK 2 HOURS**

This is a dish based on a recipe from days gone by, when no one had a fridge and you had to use the whole animal every time you slaughtered one. Any cut of pork can be used in the paella – just how it was made back then.

100ml (scant ½ cup) extra virgin olive oil
150g (5oz) pork belly, cut into lardons
150g (5oz) mini chorizo sausages
150g (5oz) smoked bacon
3 shallots, quartered
6 garlic cloves, finely chopped
1 tsp sweet smoked paprika
1 tomato, grated
1 bay leaf
0.4g saffron (see page 33 for a measuring guide)
2 sprigs of thyme
3 litres (12 cups) water
400g (2 cups) Spanish paella rice
Salt, to taste

Place a paella pan over high heat, add the olive oil and fry all the meats and shallots for 10 minutes.

Add the garlic, closely followed by the paprika and grated tomato, and cook for about 2 minutes until the oil starts to separate from the tomato paste. Add the bay leaf, saffron and thyme, pour in the water and simmer over a low heat for 1 hour.

Taste and adjust the seasoning if necessary. Add the rice and stir to distribute it evenly. Cook over a high heat for the first 10 minutes, then reduce the heat to medium and cook for a further 9 minutes, without stirring. Let it rest off the heat for 5 minutes before eating.

ARROZ A LA AMPURDANESA

SAUSAGE, RABBIT AND SAFFRON MILKCAP MUSHROOM PAELLA

SERVES 4   **PREP 15 MINUTES**   **COOK 1 HOUR 10 MINUTES**

When I was 14 years old, I joined an evening cooking course on traditional Spanish cuisine. It was my first real experience of a professional kitchen and I learned so many things on that course, this recipe being one of them. I have to say I nailed it at the time; the teacher raved about it and it's stuck in my head ever since. This is a Catalonian recipe so it has a slightly different feel – it's more meat-heavy and is cooked in lard, making it even richer. Cook it in a clay pot and you will be my hero!

120g (4oz) lard
4 garlic cloves, peeled
50g (2oz) blanched almonds
0.2g saffron (see page 33 for a measuring guide)
300g (10oz) coarse pork sausages
500g (1lb 2oz) rabbit, cut into large pieces
200g (7oz) saffron milkcap mushrooms, or other wild mushrooms
1 Spanish onion, chopped
1 tsp sweet smoked paprika
2 litres (8 cups) water
400g (2 cups) Spanish paella rice
Salt, to taste

Place a large clay pot over a medium heat, add the lard and garlic and fry for 3 minutes. Add the almonds and fry for a further 3 minutes, or until golden. Remove the garlic and almonds from the pan with a slotted spoon, then pound with a pestle and a mortar together with the saffron until you have a paste (picada). Set aside.

Add the sausages, rabbit and mushrooms to the pan and fry for 8 minutes until golden. Add the onion and fry for 5 minutes until golden. Sprinkle in the paprika, then pour in the water and the picada paste you made earlier. Bring to a gentle boil, then reduce the heat and let it simmer for 30 minutes.

Add the rice and give it a good stir, distributing it evenly, then taste the liquid and adjust the seasoning if necessary. Cook over a high heat for the first 10 minutes, then reduce to low and cook for another 9 minutes, without stirring. Let it rest off the heat for 5 minutes before eating.

ARROZ AL HORNO

BAKED MEATY RICE

SERVES 4   **PREP 30 MINUTES, PLUS SOAKING**   **COOK 2³/4 HOURS / 30 MINUTES**

This dish is arguably the most eaten rice dish in the region of Valencia (not Paella Valenciana, contrary to what most people would expect). Throughout Spain, we are addicted to eating a very traditional, soul-warming hot pot, or cocido. Each region makes it slightly differently but essentially it's the same across the board. This dish is cooked in a very large pot and always results in having leftovers that are turned into different dishes or tapas depending on the region: pringá in Andalusia, croquetas in Madrid, canelones in Catalonia... and arroz al horno in Valencia. It is outstanding in flavour, and since there is no shortcut to making a really good arroz al horno, I am obliged to give you the recipe of our soon-to-be world-famous Spanish hot pot. I hope you enjoy it!

FOR THE COCIDO (HOT POT)

- 500g (3 cups) dried chickpeas (garbanzo beans), soaked in water for 24 hours
- 6 litres (24 cups) water
- 4 chicken legs
- 1 bone of Spanish ham, or 2 bones with marrow
- 700g (1½lb) beef shin, in one piece
- 50g (2oz) dried pork fat (tocino) or dried pancetta
- 2 smoked chorizos
- 2 bay leaves
- 1 Spanish black pudding
- 3 carrots, peeled
- 1 celery stick
- 1 parsnip, peeled
- 1 onion, peeled
- 1 yellow turnip
- 1 whole head of garlic, cloves peeled
- 2 potatoes, peeled
- 200g (7oz) fideos (thin angel hair pasta)

MEAL ONE: SPANISH HOT POT

First make the cocido. Drain the soaked chickpeas and then wrap them loosely in a muslin cloth to hold them together. Add to a large stockpot (about 10 litres/2½ gallons in volume), then pour in the water and add the chicken legs, ham bones, beef shin, pork fat, smoked chorizo and bay leaves. Place over a high heat and bring to the boil, then use a ladle to skim any foam from the top of the liquid. Reduce the heat and leave to simmer over a medium heat for 1 hour.

Add the black pudding, carrots, celery, parsnip, onion, turnip and garlic cloves and simmer for another hour, skimming the fat that floats to the surface with the ladle.

Add the potatoes and simmer for another 40 minutes, or until the potatoes and chickpeas are fully cooked.

INGREDIENTS AND METHOD CONTINUED OVERLEAF

FOR THE ARROZ

120ml (½ cup) olive oil
2 dried ñora peppers
3 tomatoes
1 whole head of garlic, sliced in
    half horizontally
200g (7oz) potatoes, peeled and
    cut into large chunks
1 tsp sweet smoked paprika
0.3g saffron (see page 33 for
    a measuring guide), ground
    in a pestle and mortar
1 litre (4 cups) cocido broth
    (see previous page)
400g (2 cups) Spanish paella rice
Salt and black pepper, to taste

LEFTOVERS FROM THE COCIDO

100g (3½oz) smoked pancetta
100g (3½oz) boneless chicken
    drumsticks
70g (2½oz) chorizo, cut into thick
    slices
50g (2oz) Spanish black pudding,
    cut into thick slices
100g (3½oz) beef shin, roughly
    chopped
100g (3½oz) chickpeas (garbanzo
    beans)
1 bone with marrow

Use a slotted spoon to remove all the meats and vegetables, remove the cloth of chickpeas, then transfer to a large serving dish and keep warm. Reserve 1 litre (4 cups) of the broth for the second meal, then bring the broth to the boil, add the fideos and cook for 4 minutes, or according to the packet instructions. Serve the soup in bowls and let everyone help themselves to the rest of the ingredients. It should look like a feast! Reserve the leftovers.

MEAL TWO: BAKED MEATY RICE

When you are ready to make the arroz, preheat the oven to 200°C/400°F/gas mark 6.

Put a large clay pot or casserole dish over a high heat and pour in the olive oil and add the ñora peppers. Halve 2 of the tomatoes and add to the pan with the halved head of garlic, then cook for 4 minutes. Add the potatoes and brown them for a further 4 minutes.

Add the paprika and grate the remaining tomato into the pan. Cook for about 2 minutes until the oil starts separating from the tomato paste. Add the ground saffron, followed by the cocido broth and leftovers, and bring it to the boil. Season with salt and pepper, add the rice and stir to distribute it evenly through the pan.

Cook over a high heat for 5 minutes, then transfer to the oven for a further 15 minutes. Let it rest for 5 minutes before serving.

ARROZ MELOSO DE SECRETO IBÉRICO Y CERVEZA

PORK SHOULDER AND BEER MELLOW RICE

SERVES 4   PREP 20 MINUTES   COOK 1 HOUR 30 MINUTES

The reason I cook this dish so often at home midweek is because it uses ingredients that are easy to grab from the supermarket. As with many recipes where alcohol is added, an intensely fragrant stock is formed, giving this dish a wow factor with minimal effort. If you're in Spain, try making this with our speciality Ibérico pork – it will make this dish even better!

90ml (⅓ cup) extra virgin olive oil
600g (1lb 5oz) pork shoulder, cut into 2cm (¾in) pieces
1 carrot, diced
1 red (bell) pepper, deseeded and diced
1 leek, cut into 3cm (1¼in) rings
6 garlic cloves, finely chopped
1 clove
Pinch of dried oregano
4 black peppercorns
1 bay leaf
1 tsp sweet smoked paprika
1 tomato, grated
1 x 330ml (11fl oz) can of lager
2 litres (8 cups) water
0.3g saffron (see page 33 for a measuring guide), ground in a pestle and mortar
320g (1½ cups) Spanish paella rice
Salt, to taste

Heat the olive oil in a large pot over a high heat. Season the pork, add to the pan and brown for about 4 minutes on all sides. Add the carrot, pepper and leek and fry for 10 minutes, stirring frequently, until golden.

Add the garlic, clove, oregano, black peppercorns and bay leaf, closely followed by the paprika and grated tomato. Reduce down for 2 minutes until the oil starts to separate from the tomato.

Carefully pour in the can of beer and give it a good stir to deglaze the bottom of the pan. Let it reduce down for 2 minutes, then pour in the water. Sprinkle over the saffron and let it simmer over a medium-low heat for about 1 hour to form a very rich stock and to allow the meat to soften. Taste the stock and adjust the seasoning if necessary. There should be about 1.2 litres (5 cups) left in the pan.

Add the rice and cook over a medium heat for 10 minutes, then over a low heat for a final 8 minutes, stirring frequently to let the rice release starch and thicken the stew. Enjoy immediately.

ARROZ MELOSO DE LACÓN AHUMADO Y ESPÁRRAGOS

SMOKED HAM HOCK AND ASPARAGUS MELLOW RICE

SERVES 4   PREP 1 HOUR   COOK 3 HOURS 40 MINUTES

This is one of my favourite recipes in the book. The smokiness combined with the collagen and fat released through the long and slow cooking of the ham hock is heaven.

FOR THE HAM HOCK STOCK
1 carrot, halved
1 onion, quartered
4 garlic cloves, peeled but left whole
1 celery stick, halved
1 bay leaf
1 large smoked ham hock
Ends and peelings of asparagus (see below)
3 litres (12 cups) water
0.4g saffron (see page 33 for a measuring guide)

FOR THE RICE
160ml (generous ⅔ cup) extra virgin olive oil
4 garlic cloves, sliced
1 tsp sweet smoked paprika
1 tomato, grated
360g (1¾ cups) Spanish paella rice
150ml (generous ⅔ cup) good-quality white wine
Bunch of green asparagus spears, peeled and halved
1 sprig of oregano

Start by making the stock. Place all the ingredients in a large stockpot. Bring to the boil, then reduce the heat and simmer for 3 hours. Remove the meat from the pot and set aside to cool. When cool enough to handle, pull the meat off the bone, and shred into chunks. Carefully strain the remaining liquid and discard the vegetables – you should have about 2 litres (8 cups) of stock. Crumble the saffron into the pot and keep warm.

Heat the olive oil in a paella pan over a high heat, add the garlic and sauté until it gets a bit of colour. Add the paprika, closely followed by the tomato, and cook for 2 minutes until the oil starts to separate from the tomato paste. Add the rice and stir together for a couple of minutes, making sure all the rice gets coated with the oil. Pour in the white wine to deglaze the bottom of the pan.

Add the 2 litres (8 cups) of hot stock and the reserved ham to the pot and give it all a good stir. Taste and adjust the seasoning if necessary. Cook over a high heat for 10 minutes, then add the asparagus and oregano sprig and continue cooking over a low heat for a further 6 minutes, stirring frequently. Serve immediately and enjoy!

ARROZ DE CODORNIZ Y ALMENDRAS

QUAIL, RED PEPPER AND ALMOND PAELLA

SERVES 4　　**PREP 10 MINUTES**　　**COOK 45 MINUTES**

Game works really well in paella. I think most of us have come to terms with the fact that we should be eating meat less often, and choosing better-quality meat from high-welfare animals. Partridge, pheasant and guinea fowl all work wonders in paella, so don't hold back. An unusual ingredient in this paella is the almonds. I have experimented a lot with paellas (as you can imagine by now) and after trying almonds on one occasion with chicken, I discovered they work a treat with any bird.

1.5 litres (6 cups) chicken stock (see page 158 for homemade)
0.4g saffron (see page 33 for a measuring guide)
160ml (generous ⅔ cup) light olive oil
2 quails, cut in half
1 red (bell) pepper, deseeded and cut into strips
50g (2oz) blanched almonds
3 garlic cloves, grated
1 tsp sweet smoked paprika
2 tomatoes, grated
440g (2¼ cups) Spanish paella rice
1 tbsp dried thyme
175ml (¾ cup) good-quality white wine
Salt and pepper, to taste

Heat the chicken stock in a saucepan over the lowest heat and crumble in the saffron. Keep warm over the lowest setting.

Heat the oil in a large paella pan over a medium heat. Season the quail halves with salt, then add to the pan with the red pepper. Fry for 6 minutes until you get a caramelized golden colour on all sides. Add the almonds and fry for 1 minute.

Add the garlic, closely followed by the paprika and grated tomatoes, and cook for about 2 minutes until the oil starts to separate from the tomato paste. Add the rice and stir together for a couple of minutes, making sure all the rice gets coated with the oil.

Pour in the wine to deglaze the pan, scraping up all the bits at the bottom of the pan. Carefully add the hot stock to the pan and give it a good stir to distribute the rice evenly. Taste and adjust the seasoning if necessary. Cook over a high heat for 10 minutes, then reduce the heat to medium and cook for a further 9 minutes, without stirring. Let it rest off the heat for 5 minutes before eating. ¡Buen provecho!

ARROZ DE TUETANO Y FILETE DE TERNERA

BONE MARROW AND STEAK PAELLA

SERVES 3 **PREP 10 MINUTES** **COOK 45 MINUTES**

This recipe is an example of a style of paella that is becoming more and more popular. It involves adding any ingredient you fancy on top of your paella, one that would never usually belong inside of it, such as steak. The idea is that the rice (just 200g/1 cup here) is simply a garnish for the steak and bone marrow.

1.2 litres (6 cups) chicken stock (see page 158 for homemade)
0.2g saffron (see page 33 for a measuring guide)
80ml (⅓ cup) extra virgin olive oil, plus extra for drizzling
1 large bone marrow, split in half lengthways
350g (12oz) aged sirloin steak (remove the steak from the fridge at least 2 hours before cooking to bring it to room temperature)
3 garlic cloves, finely chopped
1 tsp sweet smoked paprika
1 small tomato, grated
200g (1 cup) Spanish paella rice
1 sprig of rosemary
Salt and pepper, to taste

Pour the chicken stock into a small saucepan, crumble in the saffron and place over a high heat until the stock reduces by a third. Keep warm over the lowest setting.

Heat the olive oil in a paella pan over a medium heat, add the marrow bones, cut side down, and fry for 10 minutes. Using a pair of tongs to hold the steak, sear the fatty edge for about 3 minutes until nicely caramelized. Set aside.

Turn the marrow bones cut side up and push them to the sides of the pan. Add the garlic, sweet smoked paprika and the grated tomato. Cook for about 2 minutes until the oil starts to separate from the tomato. Add the rice and stir, making sure the rice gets coated with the oil. Add the hot stock to the pan and give it a good stir to distribute. Taste and adjust the seasoning if necessary. Cook over a high heat for 10 minutes, then give it a shake to flatten the paella, lay the rosemary on top and continue to cook over a low heat for a further 8 minutes, without stirring.

Generously season the steak on both sides and drizzle a very hot pan with a little olive oil. Fry for 2½ minutes on each side. Transfer to the top of your paella and let it rest for 4 minutes, then move to a chopping board and slice the steak into 1cm (½in) slices. Return the steak slices to the top of the paella and enjoy immediately.

ARROZ DE COSTILLA, ALCACHOFA Y HABITAS TIERNAS

BROAD BEAN, ARTICHOKE AND PORK RIB PAELLA

SERVES 3   PREP 30 MINUTES   COOK 45 MINUTES

Pork (and all its cuts) works just beautifully in paella. Here the three main ingredients give the dish so much flavour, while the green pepper is only used in small amounts as its flavour can overpower the other ingredients.

1 litre (4 cups) chicken stock (see page 158 for homemade)
0.3g saffron (see page 33 for a measuring guide)
90ml (⅓ cup) extra virgin olive oil
300g (10oz) pork spare ribs
1 small green (bell) pepper, deseeded and roughly chopped
3 artichokes, halved
1 whole head of garlic, cloves separated and peeled
Large handful of broad (fava) beans (can be frozen)
1 tsp sweet smoked paprika
1 tomato, grated
330g (1½ cups) Spanish paella rice
Salt, to taste

Heat the chicken stock in a saucepan over the lowest heat and crumble in the saffron. Keep warm over the lowest setting.

Place a paella pan over a medium heat and add the olive oil and ribs. Fry for 10 minutes on all sides until golden. Add the green pepper, artichokes and garlic and cook for 5 minutes, then add the broad beans and cook for another minute.

Add the paprika and grated tomato and reduce down for 2 minutes until the oil starts separating from the tomato paste. Add the rice and stir all together for a couple of minutes, making sure the rice gets coated with the oil.

Carefully add the hot stock to the pan and give it a good stir to distribute the rice evenly. Taste the stock and adjust the seasoning if necessary. Cook over a high heat for 10 minutes, then reduce the heat to low and cook for 9 minutes, without stirring. Let it rest off the heat for 5 minutes before eating.

ARROZ DE ALITAS, CIRUELAS PASAS Y JEREZ DULCE

CHICKEN WING, SHERRY AND PRUNE PAELLA

SERVES 4   **PREP 20 MINUTES**   **COOK 45 MINUTES**

This paella is inventive yet not unusual in terms of Spanish flavours. I have taken familiar and beloved combinations of ingredients and paella-ized them. I invite you to do the same with any flavours you know and love, using the principles of cooking paella. Meaty, with sweetness from the prunes and sherry – this is one where the socarrat becomes more glazed than usual. What's not to like?!

1.6 litres (6 cups) chicken stock (see page 158 for homemade)
0.3g saffron (see page 33 for a measuring guide)
100g (3½oz) prunes
100ml (scant ½ cup) extra virgin olive oil
500g (1lb 2oz) chicken wings, jointed
½ Spanish onion, finely chopped
6 garlic cloves, finely chopped
1 tbsp sweet smoked paprika
1 large tomato, grated
440g (2¼ cups) Spanish paella rice
150ml (generous ⅔ cup) sweet sherry
3 sprigs of thyme
Salt and pepper, to taste

Heat the chicken stock in a saucepan over the lowest heat and crumble in the saffron. Add the prunes and keep warm over a very low heat.

Heat the olive oil in a paella pan over a high heat and add the chicken wings. Season with salt and fry for 10 minutes until well browned on all sides. Add the onion and fry for about 5 minutes, or until golden in colour.

Add the garlic, closely followed by the sweet smoked paprika and the grated tomato, and cook for about 2 minutes until the oil starts to separate from the tomato paste. Add the rice and stir all together for a couple of minutes, making sure the rice gets coated with the oil and sears.

Pour in the sherry and allow it to reduce completely, then add the hot stock to the pan and give it a good stir to distribute the rice evenly. Season with black pepper, then taste the stock and adjust the seasoning if necessary. Cook over a high heat for 10 minutes, then scatter the sprigs of thyme around the pan and give it a good shake to flatten the paella. Continue to cook over a low heat for a further 8 minutes, without stirring. Let it rest off the heat for 5 minutes before eating.

ARROZ DE SHIITAKES, ESPÁRRAGOS Y JAMÓN IBÉRICO

IBÉRICO HAM, SHIITAKE AND GREEN ASPARAGUS PAELLA

SERVES 4   **PREP 15 MINUTES**   **COOK 45 MINUTES**

The flavours of this paella work together in any dish; on this occasion the paella is just the medium. In Spain we eat this combination of ingredients often, stir-fried, in scrambled eggs, as a tapa...

1.5 litres (6 cups) mushroom stock (see page 162 for homemade)
0.4g saffron (see page 33 for a measuring guide)
3 tbsp light soy sauce
160ml (generous ⅔ cup) extra virgin olive oil
200g (7oz) green asparagus spears
300g (10oz) shiitake mushrooms
3 garlic cloves, peeled and halved lengthways
1 tsp sweet smoked paprika
2 tomatoes, grated
440g (2¼ cups) Spanish paella rice
1 sprig of rosemary
100g (3½oz) Ibérico ham, very thinly sliced
Salt, to taste

Warm the mushroom stock in a saucepan. Crumble in the saffron, add the soy sauce and keep warm over the lowest heat.

Heat the olive oil in a paella pan over a medium heat. Add the asparagus and fry for 3 minutes, then remove and set aside. Add the shiitake mushrooms and sauté for 5 minutes. Season with salt.

Add the garlic, closely followed by the sweet smoked paprika and the grated tomatoes, and cook for about 2 minutes until the oil starts to separate from the tomato paste. Add the rice and stir all together for a couple of minutes, making sure the rice gets coated with the oil.

Carefully add the hot stock to the pan and give it a good stir to distribute the rice evenly. Taste the stock and adjust the seasoning if necessary. Cook over a high heat for 10 minutes, then add the asparagus and rosemary sprig to the top of the rice. Give the pan a good shake to flatten the paella and continue to cook over a low heat for a further 8 minutes, without stirring. Let it rest off the heat for 5 minutes before laying some thinly sliced Ibérico ham on top and eating.

ARROZ DE POLLO, PERAS Y PANCETA
CHICKEN, PEAR AND SMOKED BACON PAELLA

SERVES 3   **PREP 30 MINUTES**   **COOK 45 MINUTES**

I went wild with this paella, which is to say I broke a few rules and loved the results! It was so delicious and decadent that when we shot it for the book and ate it afterwards, the team were amazed how different yet succulent it was. The pears are cooked in butter and caramelized with sugar (and we all know too well how good that tastes). My advice is: if something tastes good as it is, then you can make it work in a paella.

1 litre (4 cups) chicken stock
  (see page 158 for homemade)
0.3g saffron (see page 33 for a
  measuring guide)
90ml (⅓ cup) extra virgin olive oil
3 chicken thighs on the bone, skin
  on
100g (3½oz) smoked bacon lardons
2 garlic cloves, finely chopped
1 tsp sweet smoked paprika
1 tomato, grated
330g (1½ cups) Spanish paella rice
Sprig of rosemary
Salt and pepper, to taste

FOR THE PEARS
2 pears
Large knob of unsalted butter
3 tbsp caster (superfine) sugar

Start by caramelizing the pears. Peel and halve the pears. Melt the butter in a large pan over a medium heat and fry the pears for about 3 minutes on each side. Sprinkle the sugar over the pears and keep frying them over a high heat for a few minutes, flipping them from time to time until they turn a golden caramelized colour. Set aside for later.

Heat the chicken stock in a saucepan over the lowest heat and crumble in the saffron.

Heat the olive oil in a paella pan over a medium heat and add the chicken, skin side down first. Fry for about 5 minutes on each side. Add the bacon and fry for a further 5 minutes until all the meats are a roasted golden colour.

Add the garlic and the paprika, shortly followed by the grated tomato, and cook for 2 minutes until the oil starts separating from the tomato paste. Add the rice and stir for a couple of minutes, making sure the rice gets coated with the oil.

Add the hot stock to the pan and give it a good stir to distribute the rice evenly. Taste the stock and adjust the seasoning if necessary. Cook over a high heat for 10 minutes, then add the pears and the rosemary sprig and cook over a medium-low heat for the last 9 minutes, without stirring. Let it rest off the heat for 5 minutes before eating. *¡Buen provecho!*

ARROZ CALDOSO DE BATATA, CHORIZO Y ESPINACAS

CHORIZO, SPINACH AND SWEET POTATO RICE CASSEROLE

SERVES 4   **PREP 15 MINUTES**   **COOK 30 MINUTES**

When winter comes around we all crave a good stew. Soupy rice dishes are the perfect solution to warm our bellies and souls. Chorizo always adds something to a stew, and so does sweet potato – my partner Sandra is obsessed with this tuber, so it makes frequent appearances in anything we cook at home – luckily they're a match made in heaven.

2 litres (8 cups) vegetable stock (see page 163 for homemade)
0.4g saffron (see page 33 for a measuring guide)
120ml (½ cup) extra virgin olive oil
1 onion, finely chopped
500g (1lb 2oz) sweet potatoes, scrubbed and diced
100g (3½oz) chorizo, sliced
6 garlic cloves, finely chopped
1 tbsp sweet smoked paprika
2 small tomatoes, grated
300g (1½ cups) Spanish paella rice
300g (10oz) baby spinach
4 sprigs of thyme
Salt, to taste

Heat the vegetable stock in a saucepan over the lowest heat and crumble in the saffron. Keep warm over the lowest setting.

Heat the olive oil in a large pot over a medium heat and add the onion, sweet potatoes and chorizo and fry for 10 minutes.

Add the garlic, closely followed by the paprika and the grated tomato, and cook for about 2 minutes until the oil starts to separate from the tomato paste. Add the rice and stir together for a couple of minutes, making sure the rice gets coated with the oil.

Carefully add the hot stock to the pan and give it a good stir. Season to taste with salt, then cook over a high heat for 8 minutes before adding the spinach leaves and thyme sprigs. Reduce the heat to low and continue to cook for another 10 minutes, stirring constantly. Enjoy immediately.

ARROZ DE PATO Y ANGUILA

DUCK AND EEL PAELLA

SERVES 4   **PREP 30 MINUTES**   **COOK 45 MINUTES**

This is a very traditional recipe eaten in the area of Albufera, where rice grows in the wetlands. There we would always use fresh, locally sourced duck but I prefer using duck confit – the flavours of the fat and the tenderness of confit enhance the end result, in my humble opinion.

1.5 litres (6 cups) chicken stock (see page 158 for homemade)
0.4g saffron (see page 33 for a measuring guide)
100ml (scant ½ cup) extra virgin olive oil
2 duck confit legs, each cut into 2 pieces, fat reserved
500g (1lb 2oz) fresh eel, cut into large chunks
200g (7oz) runner beans, chopped into 3cm (1¼in) pieces
2 garlic cloves, grated
1 tsp sweet smoked paprika
1 large tomato, grated
440g (2¼ cups) Spanish paella rice
Small sprig of rosemary
Salt, to taste

Heat the chicken stock in a saucepan over a low heat and crumble in the saffron. Keep warm over the lowest setting.

Place a paella pan over a high heat and add the olive oil, the duck fat, the duck leg pieces and the eel. Fry for 6 minutes until browned, then remove the eel from the pan and set aside. Add the runner beans and sauté for 2 minutes; season with salt.

Add the garlic, closely followed by the paprika and grated tomato, and cook for about 2 minutes until the oil starts to separate from the tomato paste. Add the rice and stir together for a couple of minutes, making sure all the rice gets coated with the oil.

Carefully add the hot stock to the pan and give everything a good stir to distribute the rice evenly. Taste and adjust the seasoning if necessary. Cook over a high heat for 10 minutes, then place the rosemary sprig and eel pieces on top of the rice and continue to cook over a low heat for a further 8 minutes, without stirring. Let it rest off the heat for 5 minutes before eating.

ARROZ DE POLLO, ALCACHOFA E HINOJO

CHICKEN, ARTICHOKE AND FENNEL PAELLA

SERVES 2   **PREP 15 MINUTES**   **COOK 35 MINUTES**

I love a simple paella with just two or three ingredients, allowing the flavours to shine. Artichoke and fennel are two of my favourite vegetables. This recipe has the perfect balance of protein, vegetables and carbs and is one that I make often for dinner at home.

1 litre (4 cups) chicken stock
   (see page 158 for homemade)
0.2g saffron (see page 33 for
   a measuring guide)
60ml (¼ cup) extra virgin olive oil
2 chicken legs, each cut into
   3 pieces
1 artichoke (or 2 smaller ones),
   quartered
1 small fennel bulb, quartered
4 garlic cloves, finely chopped
1 tsp sweet smoked paprika
1 small tomato, grated
200g (1 cup) Spanish paella rice
Salt, to taste

Heat the chicken stock in a saucepan over a low heat and crumble in the saffron. Keep warm over the lowest setting.

Heat the oil in a paella pan over a medium heat. Season the chicken leg pieces with salt and fry for 10 minutes until lightly browned. Add the quartered artichokes and fennel to the pan and fry with the chicken for a further 6 minutes until caramelized on all sides.

Add the garlic, closely followed by the paprika and grated tomato, and cook for about 2 minutes until the oil starts to separate from the tomato paste. Add the rice and stir together for a couple of minutes, making sure all the rice gets coated with the oil.

Carefully add the hot stock to the pan and give it a good stir to distribute the rice evenly. Taste and adjust the seasoning if necessary. Cook over a high heat for 10 minutes, then reduce the heat to medium and continue to cook for a further 8 minutes, without stirring. Let it rest off the heat for 5 minutes before eating.

ARROZ DE LONGANIZA, CEBOLLA ROJA Y CHAMPIÑONES

SAUSAGE, RED ONION AND MUSHROOM PAELLA

SERVES 4   **PREP 20 MINUTES**   **COOK 40 MINUTES**

There are flavours that quite simply belong together, and these three are a great example of one of those matches. The beauty of paella compared with other famous rice dishes, such as biryani or risotto, is that it works with pretty much every ingredient you can think of. As a kid I never used to eat sausages except in hotdogs, but since I moved to the UK, where they are almost a staple food, I have discovered just how good they are – even in a paella.

2 litres (8 cups) pork stock
    (see page 157 for homemade)
0.4g saffron (see page 33 for
    a measuring guide)
120ml (½ cup) extra virgin olive oil
400g (14oz) pork sausages
2 red onions, cut into wedges
150g (5oz) small mushrooms, whole
6 garlic cloves, finely chopped
1 tsp sweet smoked paprika
1 tomato, grated
175ml (¾ cup) red wine
400g (2 cups) Spanish paella rice
A few sprigs of rosemary
Salt and pepper, to taste

Heat the pork stock in a saucepan over a low heat and crumble in the saffron. Keep warm over the lowest setting.

Heat the olive oil in a paella pan over a high heat and add the sausages, red onion and mushrooms. Fry for 8 minutes until everything is nicely caramelized, then season with salt.

Add the garlic, closely followed by the paprika and grated tomato, and cook for about 2 minutes until the oil starts to separate from the tomato paste. Add the rice and stir together for another couple of minutes, making sure all the rice gets coated with the oil. Pour in the red wine and let it bubble for a couple of minutes until it has reduced down.

Carefully add the hot stock to the pan and give it a good stir to distribute the rice evenly. Season with pepper and add the sprigs of rosemary. Taste and adjust the seasoning if necessary, then cook over a high heat for 10 minutes before reducing the heat to low and cooking for a further 9 minutes, without stirring. Let it rest off the heat for 5 minutes before eating.

ARROZ A LA INGLESA

THE LAZY PAELLA

SERVES 4   **PREP 5 MINUTES**   **COOK 40 MINUTES**

After living in the UK for 18 years, I've learned that the British want quick and easy solutions for dinner. This recipe is a super-easy midweek recipe, as the star ingredients come directly from your supermarket in easy-to-manage pieces, meaning minimal prep! Some purists would say that the use of chorizo in this recipe is controversial, but sometimes you just need to work smarter, not harder.

1.5 litres (6 cups) chicken stock (see page 158 for homemade)
0.3g saffron (see page 33 for a measuring guide)
100ml (scant ½ cup) extra virgin olive oil
500g (1lb 2oz) chicken wings
150g (5oz) mini chorizo sausages
100g (3½oz) mangetout
4 garlic cloves, finely chopped
1 tbsp sweet smoked paprika
1 large tomato, grated
400g (2 cups) Spanish paella rice
Salt, to taste

Heat the chicken stock in a saucepan over the lowest heat and crumble in the saffron. Keep warm over the lowest heat.

Heat the olive oil in a paella pan over a high heat and add the chicken wings. Fry for 5 minutes, then add the chorizo and fry for a further 5 minutes, or until golden in colour. Season with salt.

Add the mangetout and garlic, closely followed by the sweet smoked paprika and the grated tomato, and cook for about 2 minutes until the oil starts to separate from the tomato paste. Add the rice and stir all together for a couple of minutes, making sure the rice gets coated with the oil and sears.

Carefully add the hot stock to the pan and give it a good stir to distribute the rice evenly. Taste the stock and adjust the seasoning if necessary. Cook over a high heat for 10 minutes, then give it a good shake to flatten the paella, and continue cooking over a low heat for the next 8 minutes, without stirring. Let it rest off the heat for 5 minutes before eating it.

ARROZ DE ALBÓNDIGAS Y JUDÍAS VERDES

MEATBALL AND RUNNER BEAN PAELLA

SERVES 4   PREP 20 MINUTES, PLUS SOAKING   COOK 30 MINUTES

Meatballs are a favourite of so many people, particularly kids. I love making them from scratch; in Spain we add a lot more bread, egg and milk than in other countries, making them beautifully moist and soft, but they can also be bought from the supermarket, making this an easy midweek option if you are short on time.

FOR THE MEATBALLS
1 egg, beaten
Splash of milk
50g (2oz) stale bread, crumbled
200g (7oz) minced (ground) pork
2 tbsp chopped flat-leaf parsley
1 garlic clove, grated
2 tbsp pine nuts (optional)
Pinch of ground cinnamon
Salt and white pepper, to taste

FOR THE PAELLA
2 litres (8 cups) pork stock
    (see page 157 for homemade)
0.4g saffron (see page 33 for
    a measuring guide)
120ml (½ cup) extra virgin olive oil
1 Spanish onion, cut into wedges
150g (5oz) runner beans, cut into
    large pieces
5 garlic cloves, finely chopped
1 tbsp sweet smoked paprika
1 tomato, grated
400g (2 cups) Spanish paella rice

First make the meatballs. Mix the egg and milk together, add the crumbled stale bread and leave to soak for 10 minutes. Add to a bowl with the remaining meatball ingredients and knead for 1 minute. Form into 10–12 meatballs.

Heat the pork stock in a saucepan over a low heat and crumble in the saffron. Keep warm over the lowest setting.

Heat the olive oil in a paella pan over a medium heat and add the meatballs and onion wedges. Fry for 2 minutes on each side, then add the runner beans and fry for 3 minutes until browned. Season with salt.

Add the garlic, closely followed by the paprika and grated tomato, and cook for about 2 minutes until the oil starts to separate from the tomato paste. Add the rice and stir together for a couple of minutes, making sure all the rice gets coated with the oil.

Carefully add the hot stock to the pan and give it a good stir to distribute the rice evenly. Taste the stock and adjust the seasoning if necessary. Cook over a high heat for 10 minutes, then reduce the heat to medium and cook for a further 9 minutes, without stirring. Let it rest off the heat for 5 minutes before eating.

ARROZ AMB FESOLS I NAPS

PORK, WHITE BEANS AND TURNIP MELLOW RICE

SERVES 6   PREP 15 MINUTES, PLUS SOAKING   COOK 2 HOURS 40 MINUTES

Together with the Paella Valenciana and Arroz al Horno (see pages 52 and 63), this is one of the top three paellas in terms of popularity and how widely it is cooked in homes across Valencia. It is hearty, mellow and soupy and is a very popular dish to cook for local festivities in villages throughout the region.

300g (1¾ cups) dried white beans
(e.g. cannellini or haricot)
200g (7oz) pork belly
1 pork knuckle, cut in half
1 pig's trotter, cut in half
lengthways
100ml (scant ½ cup) extra virgin
olive oil
1½ tbsp sweet smoked paprika
2 tomatoes, grated
5 litres (20 cups) water
0.3g saffron (see page 33 for
a measuring guide)
2 swedes (rutabaga), cut into large
chunks
2 turnips, cut into large chunks
2 pork sausages
2 small morcilla
400g (2 cups) Spanish paella rice
Salt, to taste

Soak the white beans, pork belly, pork knuckle and pig's trotter in a large pan of cold water overnight, then drain.

Place a large flameproof casserole dish over a medium heat. Pour in the olive oil, sprinkle in the paprika and fry for 30 seconds. Add the grated tomatoes, fry for 3 minutes, then pour in the water. Add the drained white beans, pork meats, saffron and salt to taste and let it all simmer for 2 hours.

Add the swede, turnip, sausages and black puddings and simmer for a further 15 minutes. At this stage the liquid should have reduced by about half.

Taste the seasoning and adjust if necessary. Add the rice and cook it over a medium heat for 18 minutes, shaking the pot frequently to allow the rice to release its starch and thicken up the broth. Enjoy without delay!

NOTE
This would traditionally be made with edible thistle, but it's hard to find outside of Spain, so I have left it out of this recipe. If you come across it, do give it a try!

PAELLA MIXTA
MEAT AND SEAFOOD PAELLA

SERVES 4   **PREP 30 MINUTES**   **COOK 45 MINUTES**

The best of both worlds! This is the most sold paella in my restaurants because customers get a bit of everything. It is rare to find such a combo in Valencia city yet it is more popular in Alicante. This paella in particular was my grandfather's favourite.

2 litres (8 cups) shellfish stock (see page 160 for homemade)
0.4g saffron (see page 33 for a measuring guide)
120ml (½ cup) extra virgin olive oil
1 dried ñora pepper
2 tomatoes
4 large raw prawns (shrimp), shell on
2 chicken legs, each cut into 2 pieces
200g (7oz) squid, cleaned and cut into rings
6 garlic cloves, finely chopped
1 tsp sweet smoked paprika
440g (2¼ cups) Spanish paella rice
200g (7oz) mussels, cleaned and debearded
Salt, to taste

Warm the shellfish stock in a saucepan and crumble in the saffron. Keep warm over the lowest heat.

Place a paella pan over low heat and add the olive oil and ñora pepper. Fry for 3 minutes, then remove from the oil and blend to a paste with the tomatoes using a blender or food processor; set aside for later. Increase the heat to medium, add the prawns and cook on one side only for 2 minutes, then remove from the pan and set aside. Add the chicken pieces and fry for 10 minutes until golden on all sides. Finally add the squid and sauté for about 5 minutes, or until golden in colour. Season with salt.

Add the garlic, closely followed by the paprika and the tomato and ñora pepper paste. Cook for about 2 minutes until the oil starts to separate from the tomato paste. Add the rice and stir all together for a couple of minutes, making sure the rice gets coated with the oil.

Carefully add the hot stock to the pan and give it a good stir to distribute the rice evenly, then taste the stock and adjust the seasoning if necessary. Cook over a high heat for 10 minutes, then reduce the heat to low and cook for a further 5 minutes, without stirring. Add the mussels and prawns, cooked side up, and cook for a final 4 minutes. Let it rest off the heat for 5 minutes before eating.

ARROZ DE COSTILLA, COLIFLOR Y LONGANIZA

PORK RIB, SAUSAGE AND CAULIFLOWER PAELLA

SERVES 4 **PREP 30 MINUTES** **COOK 45 MINUTES**

Cauliflower is a tricky veg; so many people dislike it because of its aroma once boiled. I urge you to try it this way; I find the flavour much better when the cauliflower has been roasted, fried or grilled, which in essence it is what you are doing when cooking it in a paella.

1.5 litres (6 cups) chicken stock (see page 158 for homemade)
0.2g saffron (see page 33 for a measuring guide)
120ml (½ cup) extra virgin olive oil
700g (1½lb) pork spare ribs
300g (10oz) pork sausages
1 whole head of garlic, cloves peeled
1 small cauliflower, leaves reserved, broken into florets and stalk chopped
1 Spanish onion, finely chopped
1 tsp sweet smoked paprika
1 tomato, grated
400g (2 cups) Spanish paella rice
Salt, to taste

Heat the chicken stock in a small saucepan over a low heat, crumble in the saffron and keep warm over the lowest setting.

Heat the olive oil in an ovenproof paella pan over a high heat and add the ribs. Fry for 5 minutes, then add the sausages, garlic cloves, cauliflower florets and chopped stalk and the onion. Fry for a further 5 minutes until the ingredients are nicely browned.

Add the paprika and grated tomato and reduce down for 2 minutes until the oil starts to separate from the tomato paste. Add the cauliflower leaves and rice and stir all together for a couple of minutes, making sure the rice gets coated with the oil.

Carefully add the hot stock to the pan and give it a good stir to distribute the rice evenly. Taste the stock and adjust the seasoning if necessary. Cook over a high heat for 9 minutes while you preheat the oven to 240°C/425°F/gas mark 8.

Transfer the pan to the oven for a final 8 minutes. Remove from the oven and let it rest for 5 minutes before enjoying.

ARROZ DE CERDO Y ALCACHOFA
PORK AND ARTICHOKE PAELLA

SERVES 4   **PREP 20 MINUTES**   **COOK 40 MINUTES**

A treat of a paella with pork, red pepper, green beans and artichokes, which is very straightforward to cook. It's made with a clean and subtle pork stock that allows all the different flavours to shine.

2 litres (8 cups) pork stock
   (see page 157 for homemade)
0.4g saffron (see page 33 for
   a measuring guide)
1 pork cutlet
120ml (½ cup) extra virgin olive oil
½ red (bell) pepper, sliced
4 artichokes, quartered
1 Spanish onion, diced
150g (5oz) green beans, cut in half
8 garlic cloves, finely chopped
1 tsp sweet smoked paprika
1 tomato, grated
440g (2¼ cups) Spanish paella rice
Salt, to taste
Lemon wedges, to serve

Heat the pork stock in a saucepan over a low heat and crumble in the saffron. Keep warm over the lowest setting.

Generously season the pork cutlet on both sides. Heat the olive oil in a paella pan over a high heat. Holding it with tongs, sear and brown the fat of the pork cutlet, then cook on each side for 3 minutes. Set aside somewhere warm to rest.

Add the red pepper and artichokes to the pan and sauté for 4 minutes before adding the onion. Sauté for a further 2 minutes, then add the green beans and season with salt. Caramelize for another 3 minutes.

Add the garlic, closely followed by the paprika and grated tomato, and cook for about 2 minutes until the oil starts to separate from the tomato paste. Add the rice and stir together for a couple of minutes, making sure all the rice gets coated with the oil.

Carefully add the hot stock to the pan and give it a good stir to distribute the rice evenly. Taste and adjust the seasoning if necessary. Cook over a high heat for the first 10 minutes, then reduce the heat to medium and cook for a final 9 minutes, without stirring. Slice the pork and rest it on top of the paella while it finishes cooking.

Let the paella rest off the heat for 5 minutes before serving with lemon wedges for squeezing.

ARROZ MELOSO CON ALCACHOFAS Y JAMÓN

SERRANO HAM AND ARTICHOKE MELLOW RICE

SERVES 3   **PREP 15 MINUTES**   **COOK 45 MINUTES**

You have probably noticed that artichokes are the most commonly used vegetable in this book; this is not just because it is one of my favourite vegetables, but because it gives so much flavour to paellas. I have added another big flavour gun, jamón, which luckily these days you can find in any supermarket worldwide. It gives a fantastic taste to anything you add it to.

2 litres (8 cups) vegetable stock (see page 163 for homemade)
0.4g saffron (see page 33 for a measuring guide)
160ml (generous ⅔ cup) extra virgin olive oil
4 artichokes, quartered
120g (4oz) serrano ham, thinly sliced
6 garlic cloves, sliced
1 tsp sweet smoked paprika
1 tomato, grated
360g (1¾ cups) Spanish paella rice
100ml (scant ½ cup) white wine
1 sprig of rosemary, leaves picked

Heat the vegetable stock in a saucepan over a low heat and crumble in the saffron. Keep warm over the lowest setting.

Heat the oil in a paella pan over a high heat, add the artichokes and fry for 5 minutes until golden. Add the ham and garlic and sauté for a couple of minutes, or until the garlic gets a bit of colour.

Add the paprika, closely followed by the tomato, and cook for 2 minutes until the oil starts to separate from the tomato paste. Add the rice and stir together for a couple of minutes, making sure all the rice gets coated with the oil. Pour in the white wine to deglaze the bottom of the pan.

Carefully add the hot stock and the rosemary to the pan and give everything a good stir. Taste and adjust the seasoning and cook over a high heat for 5 minutes, then reduce the heat to low and cook for 12 minutes, stirring frequently. Serve immediately and enjoy!

SEAFOOD
PAELLAS

ARROZ DE SALMONETE Y CALAMAR

RED MULLET AND SQUID PAELLA

SERVES 4   **PREP 15 MINUTES**   **COOK 30 MINUTES**

I love a red mullet; it instantly transports me to Spain as it is a fish I ate a lot of as a kid. It has a special flavour and the head and bones make a very rich fish stock, so keep the bones if you are filleting this yourself, or ask your fishmonger to give them to you. I love this paella with a dollop of alioli.

2 litres (8 cups) fish stock made with red mullet bones (see page 159)
0.4g saffron (see page 33 for a measuring guide)
120ml (½ cup) extra virgin olive oil
4 red mullet, filleted (bones reserved for stock)
2 dried ñora peppers
2 tomatoes
500g (1lb 2oz) squid, cleaned and cut into rings
6 garlic cloves, finely chopped
1 tsp smoked paprika
440g (2¼ cups) Spanish paella rice
Salt, to taste
Alioli, to serve (see page 166 for homemade)

Heat the fish stock in a saucepan over a low heat and crumble in the saffron. Keep warm over the lowest setting.

Pour half the olive oil into a paella pan and place over a medium heat. Add the red mullet fillets, skin side down, and fry for 30 seconds. Remove and set aside.

Add the remaining oil to the pan and fry the ñora peppers over a low heat for 2 minutes. Remove from the oil and blend to a paste with the tomatoes using a blender or food processor; set aside for later.

Increase the heat to high and add the squid. Sauté for about 5 minutes, or until golden in colour. Season with salt. Add the garlic, closely followed by the paprika and the tomato and ñora pepper paste, and cook for about 2 minutes until the oil starts to separate from the tomato paste. Add the rice and stir together for a couple of minutes, making sure all the rice gets coated with the oil.

Carefully add the hot stock to the pan and give it a good stir to distribute the rice evenly. Taste and adjust the seasoning if necessary. Cook over a high heat for the first 10 minutes, then reduce the heat to medium and cook for a further 5 minutes, without stirring. Place the reserved red mullet fillets skin side up on top of the paella. Let it cook for a final 2 minutes, then rest off the heat for 5 minutes before eating.

ARROZ DEL SENYORET

NAKED SEAFOOD PAELLA

SERVES 3　　**PREP 20 MINUTES**　　**COOK 40 MINUTES**

This is the paella that you'll find on menus in most seaside paella restaurants in Spain. *Senyoret* means 'lord' in the Valencian dialect and, back in the day, the lords demanded that their food was prepared so that they wouldn't have to get their hands dirty, which is why the prawns are removed from their shells. This recipe relies heavily on the flavour of the stock, so you'll need to reduce your shellfish stock to maximize the flavour.

2 litres (8 cups) shellfish stock (see page 160 for homemade)
0.3g saffron (see page 33 for a measuring guide)
100ml (scant ½ cup) extra virgin olive oil
1 squid (about 600g/1lb 5oz in total), cleaned
2 garlic cloves, finely chopped
1 tsp sweet smoked paprika
4 tbsp salmorreta (see page 164)
330g (1½ cups) Spanish paella rice,
12 raw king prawns (shrimp) or langoustines, heads and shells removed and flesh diced
200g (7oz) monkfish tail, diced
Salt, to taste

Pour the shellfish stock into a saucepan, add the saffron and place over a medium heat until the liquid has reduced down to 1.2 litres (5 cups) – this will give you the extra intensity this dish requires.

Heat the olive oil in a large paella pan over a high heat and fry the squid for 5 minutes until golden. Add the garlic, closely followed by the paprika and the salmorreta, and cook for about 2 minutes until the oil starts to separate from the tomato paste. Add the rice and stir all together for another couple of minutes, making sure the rice gets coated with the oil.

Carefully pour the hot stock into the pan and give it a good stir to distribute the rice evenly. Taste the stock and adjust the seasoning if necessary. Cook over a high heat for 10 minutes, then add the prawn and monkfish pieces and continue to cook over low heat for a further 9 minutes, without stirring. Let it rest off the heat for 5 minutes before serving.

NOTE
You can add mussel meat or other shellfish to this rice, as long as it's removed from the shell.

ARROZ EMPEDRADO

SALTED COD, RED PEPPER AND WHITE BEAN MELLOW RICE

SERVES 4   PREP 15 MINUTES, PLUS SOAKING   COOK 45 MINUTES

It is traditional in Spain to eat this rice at Easter, when Christians avoid eating meat. Cod is a cold-water fish that has always been loved in Spain. It was traditionally fished in Atlantic waters off the coast of northern Europe and was salted on board so that it could be preserved for use all year round.

300g (10oz) salted cod
1.5 litres (6 cups) fish stock
    (see page 159 for homemade)
0.4g saffron (see page 33 for a
    measuring guide)
160ml (generous ⅔ cup) olive oil
1 red (bell) pepper, deseeded and
    cut into strips
400g (14oz) can white beans, rinsed
    and drained
4 garlic cloves, finely chopped
1 tsp sweet smoked paprika
1 large tomato, grated
360g (1¾ cups) Spanish paella rice

Start by soaking the salted cod in a large bowl of water for 24 hours. Change the water three times over the 24 hours. Remove from the water and cut into large chunks.

Pour the fish stock into a saucepan and crumble in the saffron. Keep warm over the lowest heat.

Pour the olive oil into a medium paella pan and place over a medium heat. Add the red pepper and fry for 5 minutes, then add the drained beans, garlic, paprika and grated tomato. Cook for about 2 minutes until the oil starts to separate from the tomato paste. Add the rice and stir all together for a couple of minutes, making sure the rice gets coated with the oil.

Finally, pour in the warm fish stock, increase the heat to high and cook for 5 minutes. Bring down the heat to low and add the cod chunks. Let it simmer for a further 11 minutes, stirring carefully every so often (so the cod doesn't crumble). Allow to rest for 3 minutes before enjoying.

ARROZ NEGRO

BLACK PAELLA

SERVES 4   **PREP 20 MINUTES**   **COOK 30 MINUTES**

This black-coloured rice dish is literally the sea on a plate. Cooked with prawns, squid and its own ink, it makes the perfect special occasion dish. In my family we eat this dish on 6th January, when we celebrate the gifts brought to Jesus by the three wise men. I have particularly fond memories of this dish; it was always my aunty Tata who cooked – but of course I always got into the kitchen to give her a hand.

2 litres (8 cups) shellfish stock
    (see page 160 for homemade)
0.4g saffron (see page 33 for
    a measuring guide)
120ml (½ cup) extra virgin olive oil
2 dried ñora peppers
2 tomatoes
1kg (2lb 4oz) cuttlefish, cleaned
    and cut into small strips
8 garlic cloves, peeled
1 tsp sweet smoked paprika
5 sachets of squid ink
440g (2¼ cups) Spanish paella rice
1kg (2lb 4oz) red prawns (shrimp),
    shells removed (heads left on)
Salt, to taste

Heat the shellfish stock in a saucepan over a low heat and crumble in the saffron. Keep warm over the lowest setting.

Place a paella pan over a low heat, pour in the olive oil and fry the ñora peppers for 2 minutes. Remove the peppers from the oil and blend to a paste with the tomatoes using a blender or food processor; set aside for later.

Increase the heat to high and add the cuttlefish. Sauté for about 5 minutes, or until golden in colour. Season with salt. Add the garlic, closely followed by the paprika, the squid ink and the tomato and ñora pepper paste. Cook for about 2 minutes until the oil starts to separate from the tomato paste. Add the rice and stir for a couple of minutes, ensuring the rice gets coated with the oil.

Carefully add the hot stock to the pan and give it a good stir to distribute the rice evenly. Taste the stock and adjust the seasoning if necessary. Cook over a high heat for the first 10 minutes, then reduce the heat to medium and continue cooking for another 5 minutes, without stirring. Place the prawns around the paella and shake the pan to flatten the rice. Let it cook for a final 2 minutes, then allow to rest off the heat for 5 minutes before eating.

ARROZ DE RAPE Y CHIPIRONES
BABY SQUID AND MONKFISH PAELLA

SERVES 4   **PREP 15 MINUTES**   **COOK 35 MINUTES**

This paella heavily relies on the quality of the ingredients, particularly your stock. Monkfish heads make the best fish stock in my opinion, better than any other fish bones, so it's worth making the most of them in this recipe.

2 litres (8 cups) fish stock made with monkfish head bones (see page 159)
0.4g saffron (see page 33 for a measuring guide)
120ml (½ cup) extra virgin olive oil
2 dried ñora peppers
2 tomatoes
400g (14oz) baby squid, cleaned
400g (14oz) monkfish tail, cut into chunks (heads reserved for stock)
6 garlic cloves, finely chopped
1 tsp sweet smoked paprika
440g (2¼ cups) Spanish paella rice
Salt, to taste

Heat the fish stock in a saucepan over a low heat and crumble in the saffron. Keep warm over the lowest setting.

Place a paella pan over a low heat, add the olive oil and ñora peppers and fry for 2 minutes. Remove the peppers from the oil and blend to a paste with the tomatoes using a blender or food processor; set aside for later.

Increase the heat to high and add the baby squid and monkfish tail. Fry for about 5 minutes, or until golden in colour, then remove the monkfish from the pan and set aside (leave the squid in the pan). Season with salt.

Add the garlic, paprika and the tomato and ñora pepper paste to the pan and cook for about 2 minutes until the oil starts separating from the tomato paste. Add the rice and stir together for a couple of minutes, making sure the rice gets coated with the oil.

Add the hot stock to the pan and give it a good stir to distribute the rice evenly. Taste the stock and adjust the seasoning if necessary, then cook over a high heat for 10 minutes. Scatter the monkfish tails around the pan, give it a good shake to flatten the paella and continue cooking over a low heat for a further 8 minutes, without stirring. Let it rest off the heat for 5 minutes before serving.

ARROZ MELOSO DE BACALAO Y SEPIA

COD, CUTTLEFISH AND RUNNER BEAN MELLOW RICE

SERVES 4   PREP 20 MINUTES   COOK 35 MINUTES

When I go on holiday to Spain the thing I most look forward to – and the thing that really tells me I am in holiday mode – is having a tapa of *sepia a la plancha*. Cuttlefish is the great unknown in the world of seafood and one that delivers in flavour massively. I love it and use it instead of squid whenever I can get hold of it.

2 litres (6 cups) fish stock
(see page 159 for homemade)
0.3g saffron (see page 33 for a
measuring guide)
120ml (½ cup) extra virgin olive oil
300g (10oz) cuttlefish, cleaned and
diced
300g (10oz) runner beans, cut into
3cm (1¼in) pieces
8 garlic cloves, sliced
1 tsp dried sweet pepper flakes
1 tbsp sweet smoked paprika
1 tomato, grated
380g (1¾ cups) Spanish paella rice
300g (10oz) cod loin, cut into
chunks
Salt, to taste

Pour the fish stock into a saucepan, crumble in the saffron and keep warm over the lowest heat.

Heat the olive oil in a paella pan over a high heat, add the cuttlefish and fry for 5 minutes until golden. Add the runner beans and garlic and sauté for a couple of minutes, or until the garlic gets a bit of colour.

Add the sweet pepper flakes and a minute later the paprika, closely followed by the tomato. Cook for 2 minutes until the oil starts to separate from the tomato paste. Add the rice and stir all together for a couple of minutes, making sure all the rice gets coated with the oil.

Carefully add the hot stock to the pan and give it a good stir – taste and adjust the seasoning if necessary. Cook over a medium heat for the first 10 minutes, then add the cod chunks, reduce the heat to low and cook for a further 12 minutes, stirring frequently. Serve immediately.

NOTE
Cuttlefish ink is precious, so if you're lucky enough to get some when you buy the cuttlefish, then I urge you to add it just before the rice. Your paella will look dark grey-brown at the end but the flavour will be sublime.

FIDEUÀ

SEAFOOD PAELLA MADE WITH PASTA

SERVES 4   **PREP 15 MINUTES**   **COOK 20 MINUTES**

Fideuà is essentially a paella made with pasta instead of rice; fideos is the short thin pasta used for this but you can make your own by breaking any long thin pasta into 2cm (¾in) pieces. Like paella it requires a big paella pan, but I promise that this recipe works in a large frying pan too. Although I'm a professional chef, I'm also an experienced home cook so I've worked out all the shortcuts for best results. This recipe is not only absolutely delicious, it's quick too. If well executed I am certain you'll become as addicted to it as I am.

1 litre (4 cups) fish stock
(see page 159 for homemade)
0.3g saffron (see page 33 for a
measuring guide)
120ml (½ cup) extra virgin olive oil
400g (14oz) fideos (or other thin,
short pasta)
1 dried ñora pepper
1 tomato
500g (1lb 2oz) squid, cleaned and
cut into strips
4 garlic cloves, finely chopped
1 tbsp sweet smoked paprika
10 prawns (shrimp)
Salt, to taste
Alioli, to serve (see page 166 for
homemade)

Heat the fish stock in a saucepan over a low heat and crumble in the saffron. Keep warm over the lowest setting.

Heat 50ml (scant ¼ cup) of the olive oil in a paella pan over a medium heat and fry the pasta, stirring constantly for around 2 minutes, or until it turns golden. Remove the pasta from the pan and set aside.

Add the remaining oil to the pan and fry the ñora pepper over a low heat for 2 minutes. Remove the pepper from the oil and blend to a paste with the tomato using a blender or food processor; set aside for later.

Increase the heat to high, add the squid to the pan and sauté for about 5 minutes, or until golden in colour. Season generously with salt. Add the garlic, closely followed by the paprika and the tomato and ñora pepper paste and cook for about 2 minutes until the oil starts to separate from the tomato paste.

Add the hot stock to the pan. Taste and adjust the seasoning, then add the pasta, give it a good stir and cook over a high heat for 3 minutes. Add the prawns and cook for a further 3 minutes, without stirring, until the bottom has formed a crispy socarrat. Enjoy with a good dollop of alioli.

ARROZ CALDOSO DE LANGOSTA

SOUPY RICE WITH LOBSTER

SERVES 4   **PREP 20 MINUTES**   **COOK 40 MINUTES**

This dish is a jewel in Spanish cuisine. For many it is the king of all rice dishes and you can understand why. Although soupy rice dishes may be perceived as more warming than a classic paella, and therefore something we would have over winter, the reality is that this dish is so popular that you will find it all across Spain, at any time of year, at all sorts of restaurants. This is the dish I chose to celebrate the birth of my first son.

2.5 litres (10 cups) shellfish stock (see page 160 for homemade)
0.4g saffron (see page 33 for a measuring guide)
150ml (generous ⅔ cup) extra virgin olive oil
2 dried ñora peppers
2 lobsters, heads halved, claws separated and tails cut into 2cm (1in) pieces
1 dried cayenne chilli pepper
2 small tomatoes
500g (1lb 2oz) squid, cleaned and roughly chopped
5 garlic cloves, finely chopped
1 tbsp sweet smoked paprika
300g (1½ cups) Spanish paella rice
Salt, to taste

Heat the shellfish stock in a saucepan over a low heat and crumble in the saffron. Keep warm over the lowest setting.

Place a paella pan over a low heat and add the olive oil, the ñora peppers and the lobster. Fry for 2 minutes, then remove the lobster from the pan and set aside. Transfer the ñora pepper to a blender with the cayenne chilli and tomatoes and blitz to a paste; set aside.

Increase the heat to high and add the squid to the pan. Sauté for about 7 minutes, or until golden in colour. Season with salt.

Add the garlic, closely followed by the paprika and the tomato and ñora pepper paste, and cook for about 2 minutes until the oil starts to separate from the tomato paste. Add the rice and stir for a couple of minutes, making sure all the rice gets coated with the oil.

Carefully add the hot stock to the pan and give it a good stir to distribute the rice evenly. Taste and adjust the seasoning if necessary. Cook over a high heat for the first 8 minutes, then add the lobster, reduce the heat to low and continue to cook for another 10 minutes, stirring constantly. Enjoy immediately.

ARROZ DE PULPO Y MEJILLONES

OCTOPUS AND MUSSEL PAELLA

SERVES 4   **PREP 30 MINUTES**   **COOK 1 HOUR**

I will always remember the answer a guest gave me when I was trying to convince him to try our octopus – he quickly interrupted me by saying: 'too many tentacles for my liking,' which I found very amusing. But jokes aside, octopus is a wonderul ingredient; it gives a fantastic flavour and is very meaty – a pleasure to bite into.

1 litre (4 cups) shellfish stock
(see page 160 for homemade)
1.5 litres (6 cups) water
1 small whole octopus (600g/1lb 5oz), cleaned
300g (10oz) mussels, cleaned and debearded
120ml (½ cup) extra virgin olive oil
½ red (bell) pepper, chopped
6 garlic cloves, finely chopped
1 tbsp sweet smoked paprika
1 tomato, grated
400g (2 cups) Spanish paella rice
Salt, to taste

Pour the shellfish stock and water into a large pot and bring to the boil over a high heat. When it comes to the boil, submerge the cleaned octopus, reduce the heat and let it simmer over a medium heat for about 20 minutes. Remove the octopus from the water with a pair of tongs and place on a chopping board. Slice up into individual tentacles and roughly chop the head, discarding the beak.

Add the mussels to the simmering shellfish stock and cook for 2 minutes, or until they all open (discard any that remain closed). Remove them with a slotted spoon, then pick the meat from the shells and set aside for later.

Heat the olive oil in a paella pan over a medium heat, add the octopus pieces and fry for 5 minutes on all sides until golden. Add the red pepper and fry for a further 5 minutes. Add the garlic, closely followed by the paprika and the grated tomato. Cook for 2 minutes until the oil starts to separate from the tomato paste. Add the rice and stir for a couple of minutes, making sure all the rice gets coated with the oil.

Add the hot stock and give it a good stir to distribute the rice evenly. Taste and adjust the seasoning if necessary. Cook over a high heat for 10 minutes, then reduce the heat to low and cook for a final 9 minutes, without stirring. Let it rest off the heat for 5 minutes before enjoying.

ARROZ MELOSO DE BONITO Y CALAMARES

TUNA, SQUID AND RED PEPPER MELLOW RICE

SERVES 4   PREP 20 MINUTES   COOK 35 MINUTES

Tuna is one of the most consumed fish in the world and in Spain we catch it both in the north and the south of our country. The reason why we love eating it raw in sushi and tartare is because in its raw form it is silky and delicious, but if overcooked becomes dry and grainy. Always add your tuna at the end, just before serving, to make sure is *just* cooked and still moist when you put it in your mouth.

2 litres (8 cups) fish stock (see page 159 for homemade)
0.3g saffron (see page 33 for a measuring guide)
1 tbsp katsuobushi smoked tuna flakes (optional)
120ml (½ cup) extra virgin olive oil
300g (10oz) squid, cleaned and diced
1 red (bell) pepper, deseeded and diced
8 garlic cloves, sliced
1 tbsp sweet smoked paprika
1 tomato, grated
380g (1¾ cups) Spanish paella rice
400g (14oz) fresh yellowfin tuna, cut into chunks
Salt, to taste

Pour the fish stock into a saucepan, crumble in the saffron and katsuobushi (if using) and warm over the lowest heat.

Meanwhile, heat the olive oil in a pot over a high heat, then add the squid and red pepper and fry for 5 minutes until golden. Add the garlic and sauté for a couple of minutes, or until it gets a bit of colour.

Add the paprika, closely followed by the tomato, and cook for 2 minutes until the oil starts to separate from the tomato paste. Add the rice and stir all together for a couple of minutes, making sure all the rice gets coated with the oil.

Carefully add the hot stock to the pot and give it a good stir. Taste the stock and adjust the seasoning if necessary. Cook over a medium heat for 10 minutes, then lower the heat and cook for a further 8 minutes, stirring frequently. Turn off the heat and gently fold in the pieces of tuna. Allow it to cook in the residual heat of the paella for 2 minutes before serving. Enjoy!

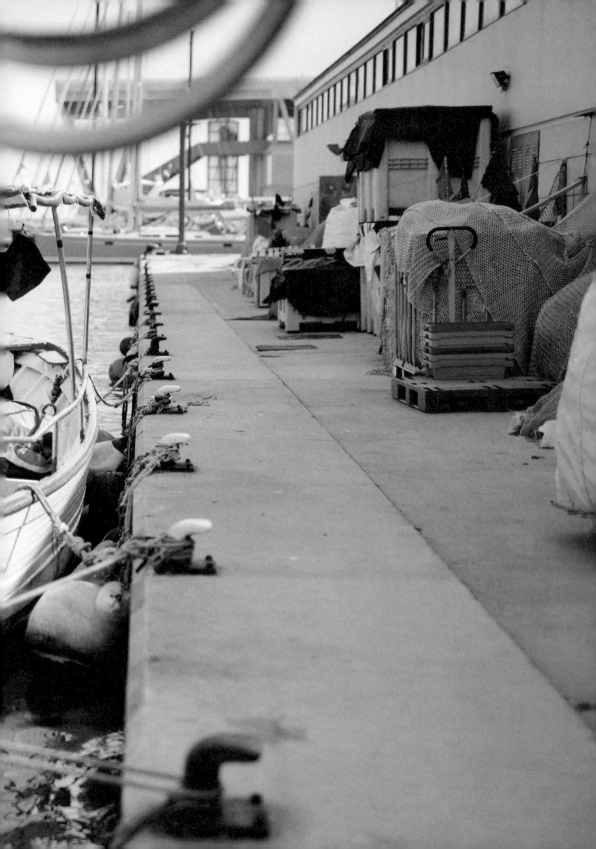

ARROZ DE CIGALAS, GAMBAS Y ALMEJAS

SHELLFISH PAELLA

SERVES 4   **PREP 20 MINUTES**   **COOK 40 MINUTES**

I confess I am a lover of shellfish above all things. I know it's pricey and that is the reason we eat it less often, but when we do, it feels really special. The beauty of paella is that you can pretty much use any ingredients, but if I had to choose one style of paella over any other I would go for a shellfish paella made with a rich and intense shellfish stock. This is a show stopper!

2 litres (8 cups) shellfish stock (see page 160 for homemade)
0.4g saffron (see page 33 for a measuring guide)
120ml (½ cup) extra virgin olive oil
2 dried ñora peppers
2 tomatoes
300g (10oz) squid, cleaned and roughly chopped
8 garlic cloves, finely chopped
1 tsp sweet smoked paprika
440g (2¼ cups) Spanish paella rice
250g (9oz) clams, cleaned
500g (1lb 2oz) prawns (shrimp), heads and shells removed
500g (1lb 2oz) langoustines
Salt, to taste

Heat the shellfish stock in a saucepan over a low heat and crumble in the saffron. Keep warm over the lowest setting.

Heat the olive oil in a paella pan and fry the ñora peppers over a low heat for 2 minutes. Remove the peppers from the oil and blend to a paste with the tomatoes using a blender or food processor; set aside for later.

Increase the heat to high, add the squid to the pan and sauté for about 7 minutes, or until golden in colour. Season with salt. Add the garlic, closely followed by the paprika and the tomato and ñora pepper paste. Cook for about 2 minutes until the oil starts to separate from the tomato paste. Add the rice and stir for a couple of minutes, making sure all the rice gets coated with the oil.

Add the hot stock to the pan and give it a good stir to distribute the rice evenly. Taste and adjust the seasoning. Cook over a high heat for the first 10 minutes, then over a medium heat for 3 minutes, without stirring. Add the clams, prawns and langoustines, gently folding them through the rice and shaking the pan to flatten the paella. Let it cook for a further 4 minutes, without stirring, then let it rest off the heat for 5 minutes before serving.

ARROZ A BANDA

PAELLA WITH FISH ON THE SIDE

SERVES 5   PREP 15 MINUTES   COOK 1 HOUR

This dish has changed so much from its humble beginnings (the recipe I am giving you) to the version you will find in so many *arrocerías* (paella restaurants) today. In my view this original version is one of the better and more natural-tasting seafood paellas as you don't use a ready-prepared stock; the broth is created by poaching the fish, and is then used to cook the rice.

FOR THE FISH AND STOCK
2.5 litres (10 cups) water
1 sea bream, cleaned and gutted
1 red snapper, cleaned and gutted
1 small monkfish tail, grey
    membrane removed
1 fennel bulb, sliced
1 onion, sliced
1 leek, sliced
1 potato, cut into 2cm (¾in) slices
3 sprigs of flat-leaf parsley
175ml (¾ cup) white wine
10 red prawns (shrimp), heads and
    shells removed, tails reserved
0.4g saffron (see page 33 for
    a measuring guide), ground
    in a pestle and mortar

FOR THE PAELLA
160ml (generous ⅔ cup) extra virgin
    olive oil
2 dried ñora peppers
2 tomatoes
300g (10oz) squid, cleaned and
    diced
6 garlic cloves, finely chopped
1 tbsp sweet smoked paprika
500g (2½ cups) Spanish paella rice
Salt, to taste
Alioli, to serve (see page 166 for
    homemade)

For the fish and stock, pour the water into a large stockpot over a high heat. Add all the ingredients except the prawns and saffron and bring to the boil, then reduce the heat and simmer for 5 minutes. Remove the fish with a slotted spoon and transfer to a large dish. Cover with foil and keep warm in a low oven until ready to serve.

Continue to simmer the stock for about 20 minutes, then strain through a colander into a clean pot. Return the stock to a low heat. Add the saffron and let it infuse for 5 minutes.

Heat the olive oil in a paella pan and fry the ñora peppers over a low heat for 2 minutes. Remove the peppers from the oil and blend to a paste with the tomatoes using a blender or food processor; set aside for later.

Increase the heat to its highest setting, add the squid and fry for 5 minutes, or until golden. Season with salt. Add the garlic, paprika and the tomato and ñora pepper paste. Cook for about 2 minutes until the oil starts to separate from the tomato paste. Add the rice and stir to distribute. Add the hot stock and give it a good stir. Taste and adjust the seasoning if necessary. Cook over a high heat for 10 minutes, then scatter the prawns around the pan and give it a good shake to flatten the paella. Continue to cook over a low heat for 9 minutes, without stirring. Turn off the heat and let it rest for 5 minutes, then serve with the poached fish and alioli on the side.

ARROZ DE GAMBAS Y MEJILLONES
CLASSIC SEAFOOD PAELLA

SERVES 4   **PREP 30 MINUTES**   **COOK 35 MINUTES**

Prawns are the most consumed seafood in the world and come in all shapes and flavours. In Spain we are privileged to have some of the best, in particular the red gamba de Denia. I am very fortunate that my partner's family own an apartment in Denia so I get to eat these prawns a couple of times a year, and it's a real treat. I hope you get to try them at least once in your life.

2 litres (8 cups) shellfish stock
  (see page 160 for homemade)
0.4g saffron (see page 33 for a
  measuring guide)
120ml (½ cup) extra virgin olive oil
2 dried ñora peppers
2 tomatoes
500g (1lb 2oz) prawns (shrimp),
  heads and shells removed
300g (10oz) squid, cleaned and
  roughly chopped
8 garlic cloves, finely chopped
1 tsp sweet smoked paprika
440g (2¼ cups) Spanish paella rice
500g (1lb 2oz) mussels, cleaned and
  debearded
Salt, to taste
Alioli, to serve (see page 166 for
  homemade)

Pour the shellfish stock into a saucepan, place over a low heat and crumble in the saffron. Keep warm over the lowest setting.

Heat the olive oil in a paella pan and fry the ñora peppers over a low heat for 2 minutes. Remove the peppers from the oil and blend to a paste with the tomatoes using a blender or food processor; set aside for later. Increase the heat to high, then add the prawns and cook on one side only for 2 minutes. Remove and set aside.

Add the squid and sauté for about 5 minutes, or until golden in colour. Season with salt. Add the garlic, closely followed by the paprika and the tomato and ñora pepper paste, and cook for 2 minutes until the oil starts to separate from the tomato paste. Add the rice and stir together for a couple of minutes, ensuring all the rice gets coated with the oil.

Add the hot stock to the pan and give it a good stir to distribute the rice evenly. Taste and adjust the seasoning if necessary. Cook over a high heat for 10 minutes, then reduce the heat to medium and cook for a further 5 minutes, without stirring.

Add the mussels and return the prawns to the pan, cooked side up. Let it cook for a final 4 minutes, without stirring, then rest off the heat for 5 minutes before serving with alioli on the side.

ARROZ DE SALMÓN Y COLIFLOR
SALMON AND CAULIFLOWER PAELLA

SERVES 4   **PREP 20 MINUTES**   **COOK 35 MINUTES**

It is rare to see a paella cooked with salmon but as it's such a popular fish in our home, I decided to try a paella with salmon and cauliflower – it was sensational. What I will point out is that salmon can easily be overcooked and consequently dries out quickly, so follow my timings carefully.

2 litres (8 cups) fish stock
  (see page 159 for homemade)
0.4g saffron (see page 33 for
  a measuring guide)
120ml (½ cup) extra virgin olive oil
2 salmon fillets, cut into large
  pieces
300g (10oz) cauliflower, broken into
  florets, core finely chopped
2 dried ñora peppers
2 tomatoes
6 garlic cloves, finely chopped
1 tsp sweet smoked paprika
440g (2¼ cups) Spanish paella rice
1 sprig of rosemary
Salt, to taste

Heat the fish stock in a saucepan over a low heat and crumble in the saffron. Keep warm over the lowest setting.

Heat half the olive oil in a paella pan over a medium heat, add the salmon fillets, skin side down, and shallow-fry for 3 minutes . Remove from the pan and set aside.

Add the remaining oil to the pan, then fry the cauliflower florets and ñora peppers over a low heat for 2 minutes. Remove the ñora peppers from the oil and blend to a paste with the tomatoes using a blender or food processor; set aside for later. Sauté the cauliflower florets for a few minutes more, then season with salt, remove from the pan and set aside.

Add the chopped cauliflower core to the pan and sauté for 2 minutes before adding the garlic, paprika and the tomato and ñora pepper paste. Cook for about 2 minutes until the oil starts to separate from the tomato paste. Add the rice and stir, making sure all the rice gets coated with the oil.

Add the hot stock to the pan and give it a good stir to distribute the rice evenly. Taste and adjust the seasoning if necessary. Cook over a high heat for 10 minutes, then reduce the heat to medium and cook for another 3 minutes, without stirring. Place the reserved salmon (skin side up), cauliflower florets and the rosemary on top of the rice and cook for a final 4 minutes. Let it rest off the heat for 5 minutes before serving.

ARROZ CALDOSO DE ANGUILA

SOUPY RICE WITH EEL

SERVES 2   **PREP 25 MINUTES**   **COOK 25 MINUTES**

I first tried this dish in a restaurant years ago and fell in love with it. It is not a dish that Spaniards come by often as it is a very regional recipe from Valencia, and of the type that doesn't travel, most likely because eels are not that easy to come by and they need to be bought and used super-fresh. When a fishmonger in Spain prepares eels for you they cut them with a bit of skin left that holds the pieces together; when you cook it you know it's just ready as the skin will break apart. The good news is that eel can be substituted by any other white firm-fleshed fish such as monkfish or hake.

80ml (⅓ cup) extra virgin olive oil
1 tomato, grated
1 small potato, cut into 1cm (½in) dice
1 clove
1 small bay leaf
1 small dried cayenne chilli pepper
1 tsp sweet smoked paprika
1 litre (4 cups) fish stock
    (see page 159 for homemade)
0.2g saffron (see page 33 for
    a measuring guide)
140g (¾ cup) Spanish paella rice
500g (1lb 2oz) fresh eel, cut into
    chunks
Salt, to taste

FOR THE PICADA
Olive oil, for frying
4 garlic cloves, peeled
8 blanched almonds
1 slice of stale bread, cut into
    1cm (½in) pieces

First make the picada. Heat a good drizzle of olive oil in a pan over a medium heat and sauté the garlic cloves, almonds and bread pieces for about 5 minutes. Once everything has a roasted golden colour, blend to a smooth paste using a pestle and mortar or blender. Set aside.

Heat the olive oil in a paella pan over a medium heat and add the grated tomato, potato, clove, bay leaf and cayenne pepper. Sauté for a few minutes until the tomato has lost most of its water. Season to taste with salt, then add the paprika followed by the picada, the fish stock and the saffron.

Bring to the boil and add the rice, then cook for 5 minutes over a high heat. Push the eel chunks into the rice and cook for a further 12 minutes over a low heat, before serving.

VEGETABLE PAELLAS

PAELLA VERDE

GREEN PAELLA

SERVES 4   **PREP 20 MINUTES**   **COOK 40 MINUTES**

Let me introduce you to my paella version of green juice. It's vegan, super-healthy, super-easy and bursting with veggie goodness! I've suggested my favourite vegetables to include but you could use any green veg. A twist on one of Spain's most famous dishes, but just as tasty.

1.6 litres (6¾ cups) vegetable stock (see page 163 for homemade)
0.3g saffron (see page 33 for a measuring guide)
120ml (½ cup) extra virgin olive oil
2 spring onions (scallions), cut into 2cm (¾in) pieces
½ head of broccoli, stem chopped and head broken into florets
3 artichokes, halved
1 courgette (zucchini), cut into 1cm (½in) slices
7 garlic cloves, finely chopped
1 tbsp sweet smoked paprika
1 tomato, grated
400g (2 cups) Spanish paella rice
100g (3½oz) baby spinach, washed
2 sprigs of flat-leaf parsley, finely chopped
2 sprigs of thyme, leaves picked
Salt, to taste

Heat the vegetable stock in a saucepan over a low heat and crumble in the saffron. Keep warm over the lowest heat.

Place your paella pan over the highest heat, pour in the olive oil and start adding your vegetables, leaving a 2-minute gap between each as they need different times to cook. Start with the courgettes, then add the artichokes, then the spring onion. Fry until all are golden in colour, which should take about 8 minutes.

Add the garlic and paprika, followed by the grated tomato, and cook for 3 minutes until reduced and the oil starts to separate from the tomato. Season with salt to taste. Add the rice and stir for 2 minutes, then pour in the hot stock. Stir briefly to distribute the ingredients evenly.

Cook over high heat for 10 minutes, stir in the broccoli, the spinach and the parsley, scatter the thyme sprigs on top and let it cook for a further 9 minutes on low heat without stirring. *¡Buen provecho!*

ARROZ DE BRÉCOL, ALCACHOFA Y AJO SILVESTRE

BROCCOLI, ARTICHOKE AND WILD GARLIC PAELLA

SERVES 3 **PREP 20 MINUTES** **COOK 40 MINUTES**

I know wild garlic is not something you'll find in the supermarket but it's an ingredient that excites me as a chef and I would like to entice you to try it. You can find it online but it grows in UK from late winter to early spring. When the season arrives I go for walks in the woodlands with my friend Dani and gather armfuls of the stuff. This combination of wild garlic, artichokes and sprouting broccoli is one of the best things in the vegetable world in my opinion. I also love a more soupy version of this dish, made by adding a little bit more stock.

2 litres (8 cups) vegetable stock (see page 163 for homemade)
0.4g saffron (see page 33 for a measuring guide)
120ml (½ cup) extra virgin olive oil
6 garlic cloves, peeled and halved lengthways
2 large artichokes (or 4 smaller ones), quartered
Bunch of sprouting broccoli
1 tbsp sweet smoked paprika
½ onion, finely chopped
1 tomato, grated
300g (1½ cups) Spanish paella rice
1 small bay leaf
100g (3½oz) wild garlic leaves
Salt and white pepper, to taste

Heat the vegetable stock in a saucepan over a low heat and crumble in the saffron. Keep warm over the lowest setting.

Pour the oil into a paella pan over a medium heat and add the garlic, artichokes and sprouting broccoli, then fry until they have taken on a golden colour. Remove the broccoli from the pan and set aside for later.

Add the paprika, onion and tomato and fry all together for about 2 minutes until the oil starts to separate from the tomato paste. Add the rice and stir together for a couple of minutes, to make sure all the rice gets coated with the oil.

Pour in the veg stock, add the bay leaf and cook over a medium-low heat for about 15 minutes. Season to taste with salt and white pepper.

Lastly, add the broccoli and wild garlic leaves and let it simmer for a couple more minutes before serving.

ARROZ CALDOSO DE ACELGAS Y JUDÍAS BLANCAS

WINTER RICE WITH HARICOT BEANS, SWISS CHARD AND ROOT VEGETABLES

SERVES 3   PREP 20 MINUTES   COOK 35 MINUTES

A lovely warming dish, similar to a casserole, perfect for a cold and rainy Sunday lunch with the family. The root vegetables work wonders to create a sweet broth with a thick consistency, while the chard adds its own distinctive taste. *¡Buen provecho!*

2 litres (8 cups) vegetable stock (see page 163 for homemade)
0.4g saffron (see page 33 for a measuring guide)
120ml (½ cup) extra virgin olive oil
4 garlic cloves, peeled and halved lengthways
1 onion, finely chopped
1 tomato, finely chopped
1 bay leaf
1 tbsp sweet smoked paprika
1 small turnip, cut into 1cm (½in) dice
1 medium parsnip, roughly chopped
300g (1½ cups) Spanish paella rice
1 medium potato, cut into 2cm (¾in) dice
400g (14oz) can haricot beans, rinsed and drained
100g (3½oz) Swiss chard, finely chopped
½ bunch of tarragon, finely chopped
Salt and white pepper, to taste

Heat the vegetable stock in a saucepan over a low heat and crumble in the saffron. Keep warm over the lowest setting.

Pour the olive oil into a paella pan set over a medium heat. Fry the garlic and onion for 10 minutes, or until golden in colour.

Add the tomato, bay leaf and paprika and fry together for about 2 minutes until the oil starts to separate from the tomato.

Add the turnip, parsnip and the veg stock and bring to the boil, then add the rice, potato, haricot beans and Swiss chard. Season to taste with salt and a pinch of white pepper and cook over a medium-high heat for 8 minutes. Reduce the heat to low, add the tarragon and cook for a further 10 minutes before serving.

ARROZ DE BERENJENA Y CALABAZA
AUBERGINE AND BUTTERNUT SQUASH PAELLA

SERVES 4   **PREP 15 MINUTES**   **COOK 35 MINUTES**

In any normal household, dinners are frequently made with whatever there is in the fridge. These are two ingredients we generally have in our home, so often they become the focus of a paella.

1.5 litres (6 cups) vegetable stock (see page 163 for homemade)
0.2g saffron (see page 33 for a measuring guide)
120ml (½ cup) extra virgin olive oil
400g (14oz) butternut squash, peeled and cut into 3cm (1¼in) pieces
1 large aubergine (eggplant), cut into 3cm (1¼in) pieces
1 onion, finely chopped
8 garlic cloves, finely chopped
1 tsp dried sweet pepper flakes
1 tbsp sweet smoked paprika
1 large tomato, grated
400g (2 cups) Spanish paella rice
2 sprigs of sage, finely chopped
Salt, to taste

Heat the vegetable stock in a saucepan over a low heat and crumble in the saffron. Keep warm over the lowest setting.

Heat the olive oil in a paella pan over a high heat. Add the butternut squash and aubergine and fry for 10 minutes until caramelized on all sides. Season with salt and add the onion, then fry for a further 5 minutes.

Add the garlic and sweet pepper flakes, closely followed by the paprika and grated tomato, and cook for about 2 minutes until the oil starts to separate from the tomato paste. Add the rice and stir together for another couple of minutes, making sure all the rice gets coated with the oil.

Carefully pour the hot stock into the pan and give it a good stir to distribute the rice evenly. Taste the stock and adjust the seasoning if necessary. Cook over a high heat for 10 minutes, then add the sage and continue to cook over a low heat for a further 9 minutes, without stirring. Let it rest off the heat for 5 minutes before serving.

ARROZ MELOSO DE PUERROS Y CALABACÍN

SOUPY RICE WITH LEEK, COURGETTE AND FRESH HERBS

SERVES 4   PREP 20 MINUTES   COOK 40 MINUTES

Two of my most-loved vegetables come together to create this rice dish. Leek gives so much flavour to the stock, the courgette gives bite to the recipe, while the herbs bring the romance, freshness and aroma. As you may have guessed, this is one of my favourites at home. Green always feels good!

1.5 litres (6 cups) vegetable stock (see page 163 for homemade)
0.2g saffron (see page 33 for a measuring guide)
120ml (½ cup) extra virgin olive oil
3 leeks, finely chopped
2 courgettes (zucchini), diced
6 garlic cloves, thinly sliced
Pinch of sweet smoked paprika
360g (1¾ cups) Spanish paella rice
50ml (scant ¼ cup) white wine
4 sprigs of basil, thinly sliced
4 sprigs of tarragon, finely chopped
Salt and white pepper, to taste
Alioli, to serve (see page 166 for homemade)

Pour the stock into a small saucepan, warm over a low heat and crumble in the saffron. Keep warm over the lowest setting.

Pour the olive oil into a large saucepan over a medium heat, add the leeks and fry for 10 minutes until they soften. Add the courgette and fry for a further 5 minutes.

Add the garlic, season with salt and fry for 5 more minutes. Add the paprika, a pinch of white pepper and the rice and fry for 2 minutes before adding the white wine. Let it bubble away and reduce before pouring in the hot stock.

Give everything a good stir and taste and adjust the seasoning if necessary. After 5 minutes reduce the heat to low and simmer for 11 minutes, stirring every couple of minutes, before adding the basil and tarragon and cooking it for a further minute. Pour a generous ladle of the rice on a plate and enjoy! Alioli is a wonderful accompaniment to this rice.

ARROZ DE TUPINAMBO, SETAS Y CASTAÑAS

WILD MUSHROOM, JERUSALEM ARTICHOKE AND CHESTNUT PAELLA

SERVES 4   **PREP 20 MINUTES**   **COOK 40 MINUTES**

As we get deep into autumn, the variety of mushrooms available in local markets multiplies, while Jerusalem artichokes, which I love, start appearing on restaurant menus. This is not a vegetable we grow much in Spain so I only discovered them when I first came to the UK 18 years ago – now I love using them in my paellas. A few shavings of chestnut to finish will make this dish feel extra special, without having to spend a fortune on truffle.

2 litres (8 cups) mushroom stock (see page 162 for homemade)
0.4g saffron (see page 33 for a measuring guide)
140ml (generous ½ cup) extra virgin olive oil
200g (7oz) Jerusalem artichokes, peeled and cut into chunks
200g (7oz) wild mushrooms, roughly torn
½ onion, finely chopped
6 garlic cloves, finely chopped
1 tsp sweet smoked paprika
1 tomato, grated
440g (2¼ cups) Spanish paella rice
A few sprigs of thyme
Salt and pepper, to taste
Fresh chestnuts, to finish

Heat the mushroom stock in a saucepan over a low heat and crumble in the saffron. Keep warm over the lowest setting.

Heat the olive oil in a paella pan over a high heat, add the Jerusalem artichoke and fry for 5 minutes. Add the mushrooms and fry for a further 4 minutes, then add the onion and fry for a few more minutes until everything is nicely caramelized. Season with salt.

Add the garlic, closely followed by the paprika and grated tomato, and cook for about 2 minutes until the oil starts to separate from the tomato paste. Add the rice and stir together for another couple of minutes, making sure all the rice gets coated with the oil.

Carefully add the hot stock to the pan and give it a good stir to distribute the rice evenly. Season with pepper and add the sprigs of thyme. Taste and adjust the seasoning, then increase the heat to high and cook for 10 minutes. Reduce the heat to medium and cook for a further 9 minutes, without stirring. Let it rest off the heat for 5 minutes. Use a truffle shaver or vegetable peeler to shave chestnuts over the top, then enjoy.

ARROZ DE ENDIVIAS, BRÉCOL Y MANZANA

CHICORY ENDIVE, APPLE AND SPROUTING BROCCOLI PAELLA

SERVES 4   PREP 20 MINUTES   COOK 40 MINUTES

I have a particular love of bitter flavours, things like frisée lettuce, chicory, cranberries, coffee and of course chocolate! To me these are ingredients that need a little help to bring out their natural sweetness and make the dish more rounded. This is a good example of how fruit can play an important role in savoury dishes.

2 litres (8 cups) vegetable stock (see page 163 for homemade)
0.4g saffron (see page 33 for a measuring guide)
140ml (generous ½ cup) extra virgin olive oil
200g (7oz) sprouting broccoli
2 chicory endives, quartered lengthways
2 apples, cored and sliced
6 garlic cloves, finely chopped
1 tsp sweet smoked paprika
1 tomato, grated
440g (2¼ cups) Spanish paella rice
1 shot of whisky (or rum)
A few sprigs of rosemary
Salt, to taste

Heat the vegetable stock in a saucepan over a low heat and crumble in the saffron. Keep warm over the lowest setting.

Heat the olive oil in a paella pan over a high heat and add the broccoli, chicory endives and apples. Fry for 10 minutes until everything is nicely caramelized (remove the broccoli from the pan after 3 minutes), then season with salt.

Add the garlic, closely followed by the paprika and grated tomato, and cook for about 2 minutes until the oil starts to separate from the tomato paste. Add the rice and stir together for another couple of minutes, making sure all the rice gets coated with the oil.

Pour in the shot of whisky and reduce slightly, then carefully add the hot stock to the pan and give it a good stir to distribute the rice evenly. Taste and adjust the seasoning if necessary.

Cook over a high heat for 10 minutes, then add the rosemary and sprouting broccoli and continue to cook over a medium heat for a further 9 minutes, without stirring. Let it rest off the heat for 5 minutes before serving.

ARROZ 'MORAO'

BEETROOT, RED ONION AND RED WINE PAELLA

SERVES 4   **PREP 20 MINUTES**   **COOK 35 MINUTES**

This is the earthiest paella in this book and I love it. I am a big fan of beetroot and red onion, not to mention red wine! This is one of the quickest paellas to prepare as the ingredients are roughly chopped and you are giving extra flavour to it by adding the red wine.

1.6 litres (6¾ cups) vegetable stock (see page 163 for homemade)
0.4g saffron (see page 33 for a measuring guide)
120ml (½ cup) extra virgin olive oil
300g (10oz) beetroot (beets), cut into large chunks
2 red onions, cut into wedges
6 garlic cloves, finely chopped
1 tsp sweet smoked paprika
1 tomato, grated
400g (2 cups) Spanish paella rice
175ml (¾ cup) red wine
A few sprigs of thyme
Salt and pepper, to taste

Pour the vegetable stock into a saucepan over a low heat and crumble in the saffron. Keep warm over the lowest heat.

Heat the olive oil in a paella pan over high heat and add the beetroot and red onion. Fry for 8 minutes until a nice brown caramelization has been achieved. Season with salt.

Add the garlic, closely followed by the paprika and grated tomato, and cook for about 2 minutes until the oil starts to separate from the tomato paste. Add the rice and stir together for another couple of minutes, making sure all the rice gets coated with the oil. Pour in the red wine and let it reduce completely.

Add the hot stock to the pan and give it a good stir to distribute the rice evenly. Season with pepper and add the sprigs of thyme. Taste the stock and adjust the seasoning if necessary. Cook over a high heat for 10 minutes, then reduce the heat to low and cook for a further 9 minutes, without stirring. Let it rest off the heat for 5 minutes before enjoying.

ARROZ DE AJETES, HABITAS TIERNAS Y APIO NABO

CELERIAC, SPRING GREENS AND BROAD BEAN PAELLA

SERVES 4   **PREP 20 MINUTES**   **COOK 35 MINUTES**

These ingredients are at their peak early in the year and make the perfect winter paella.

1.6 litres (6¾ cups) vegetable stock (see page 163 for homemade)
0.4g saffron (see page 33 for a measuring guide)
120ml (½ cup) extra virgin olive oil
300g (10oz) celeriac, peeled and cut into large chunks
200g (7oz) spring greens
70g (2½oz) broad (fava) beans
6 garlic cloves, finely chopped
1 tsp sweet smoked paprika
1 tomato, grated
400g (2 cups) Spanish paella rice
A few sprigs of oregano
Salt and pepper, to taste

Pour the vegetable stock into a saucepan set over a low heat and crumble in the saffron. Keep warm over the lowest heat.

Heat the olive oil in a paella pan over a high heat, add the celeriac and fry for 8 minutes until a nice brown caramelization has been achieved. Season with salt. Add the spring greens and broad beans and continue to fry for a further 3 minutes.

Add the garlic, closely followed by the paprika and grated tomato, and cook for about 2 minutes until the oil starts to separate from the tomato paste. Add the rice and stir together for another couple of minutes, making sure all the rice gets coated with the oil.

Carefully add the hot stock to the pan and give it a good stir to distribute the rice evenly. Season with pepper and add the sprigs of oregano. Taste the stock and adjust the seasoning if necessary. Cook over a high heat for 10 minutes, then reduce the heat to low and cook for a further 9 minutes, without stirring. Let it rest off the heat for 5 minutes before enjoying.

ARROZ EN BLEDES
SOUPY RICE WITH SWISS CHARD AND BUTTER BEANS

SERVES 6   **PREP 20 MINUTES**   **COOK 25 MINUTES**

It is a tradition to have this dish on Spanish Father's Day, on 19 March, which is also the day of San José (my mum is called María José so we would always celebrate this day with all the family as well). It's no coincidence that this is also the last day of the Valencian celebration: *Las Falles de València.*

2 litres (8 cups) vegetable stock (see page 163 for homemade)
0.2g saffron (see page 33 for a measuring guide)
100ml (scant ½ cup) extra virgin olive oil
1 swede (rutabaga), peeled and cut into large dice
15 Swiss chard leaves, leaves and stalks chopped separately
1 tsp sweet smoked paprika
1 large tomato, grated
500g (2½ cups) Spanish paella rice (I like bomba for this dish)
300g (10oz) canned butter beans, rinsed and drained
Salt, to taste

Pour the vegetable stock into a pan, crumble in the saffron and leave to infuse over a very low heat.

Heat the oil in a paella pan over a medium heat, add the swede and fry on all sides for about 8 minutes until lightly caramelized. Add the chopped Swiss chard stalks and fry for a further 5 minutes.

Add the paprika and grated tomato to the pan and keep cooking for 2 minutes until the oil starts to separate from the tomato paste. Pour in the vegetable stock and simmer for 5 minutes.

Add the rice, butter beans and chopped Swiss chard leaves and cook over a medium heat for 17 minutes, stirring frequently to prevent the beans catching on the bottom of the pan. Taste and adjust the seasoning before serving.

ARROZ DE SETAS

WILD MUSHROOM PAELLA

SERVES 4   **PREP 30 MINUTES**   **COOK 30 MINUTES**

I love mushrooms and especially picking them – it's such a great opportunity to get out of the city and spend a day in the woods. I used to go mushroom picking with my parents; now I take my own kids along with my dear friend Dani. Mushrooms and rice belong together and there is such a wide variety of mushrooms so I urge you to pick up something different in your local market and give it a try in a paella. If you can afford it, a shaving of truffle on top of this paella for a special occasion will be spectacular.

1.5 litres (6 cups) mushroom stock (see page 162 for homemade)
0.4g saffron (see page 33 for a measuring guide)
160ml (generous ⅔ cup) extra virgin olive oil
500g (1lb 2oz) wild mushrooms, e.g. oyster, chanterelle, ceps, black trumpet, shiitake
1 onion, finely chopped
6 garlic cloves, sliced
1 tbsp sweet smoked paprika
1 small tomato, grated
440g (2¼ cups) Spanish paella rice
4 sprigs of thyme
Pinch of dried oregano
Salt, to taste

Heat the mushroom stock in a saucepan over a low heat and crumble in the saffron. Keep warm over the lowest setting.

Heat the olive oil in a paella pan over a high heat, add the mushrooms and sauté for 5 minutes. Season with salt, add the onion and fry for a further 5 minutes.

Add the garlic, closely followed by the paprika and grated tomato and cook for about 2 minutes until the oil starts to separate from the tomato paste. Add the rice and stir together for another couple of minutes, making sure all the rice gets coated with the oil.

Carefully add the hot stock to the pan and give it a good stir to distribute the rice evenly. Add the thyme sprigs and dried oregano, then taste and adjust the seasoning. Cook over a high heat for 10 minutes, then reduce the heat to medium and cook for a further 9 minutes, without stirring. Let it rest off the heat for 5 minutes before eating.

STOCKS
& EXTRAS

CALDO DE CARNE

MEAT STOCK

MAKES ABOUT 3 LITRES (12 CUPS)

I commonly use this technique to make beef or pork stock, but it will work with any meat bones.

2 Spanish onions, cut into wedges
1 leek, cut into chunks
4 carrots, cut into chunks
3 celery sticks, cut into chunks
1 tomato, quartered
10 garlic cloves, unpeeled
Drizzle of olive oil
2kg (4lb 8oz) beef, pork, lamb
   or game bones, cut widthways
2 bay leaves
1 clove
10 black peppercorns
Pinch of salt
5 sprigs of tarragon
2 sprigs of rosemary
175ml (¾ cup) red wine
5 litres (20 cups) water

Preheat the oven to 210°C/410°F/gas mark 7.

Put the onion, leek, carrots, celery, tomato quarters and garlic cloves into a large roasting pan and drizzle with olive oil. Spread out the bones in a separate roasting pan. Put both pans in the oven and roast for about 1 hour, or until dark brown, tossing halfway through.

Transfer all the ingredients from both pans to a large stockpot, then put the empty pans over a high heat and deglaze with a splash of water, scraping up all the charred bits with a metal spoon. Pour this into the stockpot.

Add all the remaining ingredients to the stockpot and bring to the boil over a high heat, then reduce the heat and simmer with a lid on for about 4 hours.

Strain the stock into a clean container. Once cool, you can keep it in the fridge for up to 5 days or in the freezer for up to 3 months. Some fat will float to the top of the stock once it is cool – you can remove this easily with a spoon.

CALDO OSCURO DE POLLO
ROASTED CHICKEN STOCK

MAKES ABOUT 2.5 LITRES (10½ CUPS)

When you want to add more flavour to different dishes, the answer is often this rich and flavoursome homemade chicken stock (also called 'brown chicken stock'). Of course, there are times when we resort to the quick stock cube option, but a homemade stock will make all the difference to your paellas.

This method will work with any bird (one of my favourites to make is pheasant stock) so feel free to experiment!

1 Spanish onion, thickly sliced
2 carrots, roughly chopped
2 celery sticks, thickly sliced
1 tomato, cut into wedges
5 garlic cloves, unpeeled
1 chicken carcass, plus wings
Drizzle of olive oil
1 bay leaf
1 clove
4 black peppercorns
Pinch of salt
2 sprigs of thyme
2 sprigs of flat-leaf parsley
1 sprig of rosemary
1 shot of brandy
3 litres (12 cups) water

Preheat the oven to 210°C/410°F/gas mark 7.

Put the onion, carrots, celery, tomato and garlic cloves in a large roasting pan. Spread the pieces of chicken over the top and drizzle with oil, then roast in the oven for about 45 minutes, or until dark brown, tossing every 15 minutes.

Transfer all the ingredients from the pan to a stockpot, then put the empty pan over a high heat and deglaze with a splash of water, scraping up all the charred bits with a metal spoon. Pour this into the stockpot.

Add all the remaining ingredients to the stockpot and bring to the boil over a high heat, then reduce the heat and simmer with the lid on for about 2 hours.

Strain the stock into a clean container. Once cool, you can keep it in the fridge for up to 5 days or in the freezer for up to 3 months. Some fat will float to the top of the stock once it is cool – you can remove this easily with a spoon.

CALDO DE PESCADO

FISH STOCK

MAKES ABOUT 4.5 LITRES (19 CUPS)

This versatile stock is great for any fish dish. It is quite subtle in flavour and clean in look. Any of the following fish bones make a beautiful stock: turbot, hake, cod, monkfish, seabass, bream, sole. Avoid using oily fish such as salmon, mackerel, trout, tuna or sardines. Any good fishmonger will generally save fish bones and heads for making stock and you should be able to buy them at an affordable price.

2kg (4lb 8oz) fresh fish bones (see intro)
1 carrot, thickly sliced
2 onions, roughly chopped
5 celery sticks, roughly sliced
2 leeks, sliced
1 fennel bulb, thickly sliced
175ml (¾ cup) white wine
10 white peppercorns
1 clove
4 bay leaves
5 sprigs of tarragon
5 sprigs of flat-leaf parsley
1 tsp fennel seeds
5 litres (20 cups) water

First and foremost, make sure your fish bones are as clean as they can be. Rinse them under cold running water to make sure there is no blood and to double-check they have been properly gutted by your fishmonger.

Add the fish bones to a stockpot, then add all the remaining ingredients. Place over a high heat and let it come to the boil. Skim the froth from the surface with a ladle, then reduce the heat to medium and let it simmer gently for 30 minutes, without stirring.

Let it cool off the heat for 30 minutes before straining through a fine sieve into a clean container. You can keep it in the fridge for up to 5 days or in the freezer for up to 3 months.

CALDO DE MARISCO

SHELLFISH STOCK

MAKES ABOUT 4.5 LITRES (19 CUPS)

Shellfish in general is one of the less used ingredients in the home kitchen and it's a real shame as it holds some of the most delicious flavours. In Spain we just can't get enough of it and we import vast amounts from the UK and beyond. This stock recipe is the base for any great seafood dish or sauce.

500g (1lb 2oz) langoustines
500g (1lb 2oz) large shell-on prawns (shrimp)
3 tbsp light olive oil
3 bay leaves
1 whole head of garlic, cloves peeled
200g (7oz) onion, roughly chopped
200g (7oz) carrot, roughly chopped
200g (7oz) leek, roughly chopped
150g (5oz) celery, roughly chopped
1 tomato (optional)
1 tsp fennel seeds
1 sprig of rosemary
3 sprigs of flat-leaf parsley
1 shot of brandy
100ml (scant ½ cup) white wine
5 litres (20 cups) water
Pinch of black pepper

Firstly, remove the heads and shells from the langoustines and the prawns. Put the clean tails of the shellfish to good use, such as cooking a sensational shellfish paella.

Heat the olive oil in a stockpot over a high heat and add the langoustine heads and shells. Fry for 3 minutes, then add the bay leaves, garlic and all the vegetables and fry for a further 10 minutes, stirring frequently.

Add the fennel seeds, rosemary and parsley. Pour in the brandy and allow it to reduce, then pour in the white wine. Let it reduce down completely then add the water. Bring to the boil, then skim away the froth that rises to the surface with a ladle. Reduce the heat to low, season with pepper and simmer with the lid on for 1½ hours.

Place a colander over a large bowl or a saucepan and carefully strain the stock, then strain again, this time through a sieve lined with muslin or cheesecloth. Transfer to an airtight container. You can keep it in the fridge for up to 5 days or in the freezer for up to 3 months.

FUMET DE SETAS

MUSHROOM STOCK

MAKES ABOUT 2.5 LITRES (10½ CUPS)

I love foraging for mushrooms and every autumn I keep my eye out for them on my walks. I love a good soupy mushroom paella made with mushroom stock, which gives the dish a lovely earthy flavour. I like my mushroom dishes to taste very pure as if I was tasting and smelling the forest.

100ml (scant ½ cup) olive oil
1 large Spanish onion, thinly sliced
1 celery stick, thinly sliced, any
   fronds reserved
250g (9oz) button mushrooms,
   lightly cleaned with a damp cloth
   then thinly sliced
1 bay leaf
4 garlic cloves, lightly crushed
1 tsp fennel seeds
1 shot of brandy
3 litres (12 cups) water
50g (2oz) dried shiitake or porcini
   mushrooms
2 sprigs of thyme
Salt and pepper

Set a stockpot over a medium heat and add the olive oil, onion and sliced celery. Fry for 5 minutes, then add the button mushrooms, bay leaf and garlic and sauté for a further 10 minutes. Add the fennel seeds, season with salt and pepper, then add the brandy and allow to reduce.

Pour in the water, then add the dried mushrooms, thyme and any fronds from the celery. Simmer with the lid on for 45 minutes.

Strain through a fine sieve into a large container and store in the fridge or freezer once cool.

CALDO OSCURO DE VERDURAS
THE ULTIMATE VEGETABLE STOCK

MAKES ABOUT 4.5 LITRES (19 CUPS)

Let me introduce you to the vegetable stock that is going to transform the taste of any vegan or vegetarian dish. For most of us who eat a flexitarian diet, I think we generally struggle with the lack of depth of flavour from recipes and dishes, whether at home or in restaurants. They miss finesse, layers of flavour and mainly an incredibly satisfying sense of indulgence. This stock is going to give maximum flavour to anything you add it to: paellas, sauces and soups will never be the same again.

5 carrots
1 parsnip
1 fennel bulb
½ a bunch of celery
4 leeks, green parts only (reserve the whites for another use)
2 tomatoes
3 shallots
1 whole head of garlic, sliced in half
4 tbsp olive oil
5 litres (20 cups) cold water
6 black peppercorns
2 cardamom pods
½ tsp smoked chipotle
½ tsp fennel seeds
2 cloves
3 bay leaves
5 sprigs of flat-leaf parsley
3 sprigs of tarragon
6 sprigs of thyme
30g (1oz) dried porcini mushrooms
1 large glass of white wine
Salt

Preheat the oven to 250°C/475°F/gas mark 9.

Wash and peel the carrot and parsnip. Place the peelings in a stockpot. Remove the young leaves from both the fennel and the celery and place them in the pot too. Roughly chop all the vegetables: the green parts of the leek, tomatoes, shallots and the remaining carrot, parsnip, celery and fennel, and place it all in a large roasting pan along with the halved garlic bulb.

Drizzle the chopped vegetables with some olive oil, season with salt and place in the oven for 45 minutes, tossing them twice through the cooking process so they brown evenly.

Meanwhile, fill the stockpot with cold water and add all the spices, herbs and mushrooms. Bring it to the boil, then turn down the heat and allow it to simmer.

When the roasted vegetables are ready, deglaze the pan with the white wine, scraping up any charred bits, then tip all this into the stockpot. Simmer with the lid on over a low heat for a minimum of 2 hours and a maximum of 4 hours. Strain through a fine sieve into a large container and store in the fridge or freezer once cool.

SALMORRETA
PAELLA FLAVOUR ENHANCER

MAKES ABOUT 200G (7OZ)

The salmorreta is essentially a paste made by frying garlic, ñora peppers and tomatoes together. It is full of umami flavour and is fundamental to so many paellas. You would normally use it in place of the grated tomato – a medium tomato should be substituted with 2 tablespoons of salmorreta. This is a very useful and tasty base recipe for cooking paellas, particularly in a restaurant environment, where you don't have the time to cook a paella from scratch like you would at home. Having said that, it's not just about convenience; salmorreta has a particular taste more often found in paellas cooked in the southern province of Alicante. I like to describe it as a flavour enhancer. No paella in which you have use salmorreta will taste bland, I guarantee you that.

50ml (scant ¼ cup) extra virgin olive oil
5 garlic cloves, peeled
5 dried ñora peppers, crumbled into 2cm (¾in) pieces
3 sprigs of flat-leaf parsley, roughly chopped
3 tomatoes (about 400g/14oz), grated

Pour the oil into a small saucepan and add the garlic. Place over a medium heat and fry them for about 5 minutes until slightly golden. Add the ñora peppers and fry, stirring frequently, for a further 2 minutes, or until they start turning slightly darker in colour and you can smell their particular nutty and smoky aroma. Be careful as you don't want to burn them; like garlic they will turn bitter.

Add the parsley and fry for a minute before adding the tomatoes. Lower the heat and cook for about 45 minutes until it has reduced down into a paste.

Blend in a food processor or blender until smooth and transfer to an airtight container once cool. It will last up to 5 days if refrigerated but as this recipe makes enough for 10 portions, if you are not going to use it all, just freeze it in an ice-cube tray, ready for your next paella.

ALIOLI
GARLIC MAYONNAISE

MAKES ABOUT 200G (7OZ)

This sauce is like ketchup for us in Spain; it is undoubtedly the most consumed of all sauces and most of it is eaten on the Mediterranean coast, where it is traditionally from, with rice. Nothing beats our love of garlic, and this sauce is the epitome of it. I've given you a selection of quite distinctive styles of alioli – one 'original' recipe and three variations – all of which I love equally and use frequently.

THE ORIGINAL ALIOLI
3 garlic cloves, peeled and halved lengthways
½ tsp salt
150ml (generous ⅔ cup) extra virgin olive oil

Unless your garlic cloves are very young and fresh, it's a good idea to remove the garlic germ (the small green shoots inside the clove) as they can make the garlic taste bitter, especially if it is not being cooked, as here. Discard the germs and chop the cloves finely.

Put the chopped garlic and salt in a mortar and pound it with a pestle until you have a very, very, very (I mean it!) smooth paste.

Now you need to add the oil. You can continue using the pestle and mortar if you wish or you can transfer the garlic paste to a larger bowl and use a whisk – the taste will be the same but using a whisk will result in a lighter-coloured alioli. Start adding the oil in a very thin, slow stream, mixing all the time. The idea is to emulsify the oil with the salt and garlic paste. Keep adding the oil until it is all used up.

MILK-BASED ALIOLI

6 tbsp milk
1 tsp Dijon or English mustard
1 garlic clove
½ tsp salt
150ml (generous ⅔ cup) light olive oil

MAYONNAISE-STYLE ALIOLI

1 egg
2 garlic cloves
½ tsp salt
1 tbsp lemon juice
50ml (scant ¼ cup) vegetable oil
100ml (scant ½ cup) extra virgin olive oil

ROASTED GARLIC ALIOLI

1 whole head of garlic, roasted whole at 200°C/400°F/gas mark 6 for 20 minutes, cooled and pulp squeezed out
1 egg
½ tsp salt
1 tbsp lemon juice
150ml (generous ⅔ cup) light olive oil

For the variations, I'd recommend using the following method. Place all the ingredients, except the bulk quantity of oil, into a blender or a small jug. Blitz (or use a stick blender) to combine everything until smooth, then slowly pour in the oil in a long, thin stream until it completely emulsifies.

Troubleshooting: If you are unlucky and your alioli splits, add a splash of cold water to a clean bowl, then blitz while you slowly add the split mixture in a thin stream (just as you did with the olive oil). It should come together again into a smooth alioli.

YOUR PAELLA

SERVES: **PREP:**   **COOK:**

Each of us favours different ingredients and we all have various equipment and pans at home that will give a degree of results when cooking. This is the place where I want you to jot down your own experiences of cooking those first paellas, what you liked and didn't like, the ratios of rice and stock you used and the results achieved. And even how you nailed the perfect socarrat. These notes will help you improve time on time so that you can nail YOUR PAELLA, famous between your family and friends.

INGREDIENTS   **METHOD**

....

....

....

....

....

....

....

....

....

....

....

....   **NOTES**

....

....

....

INDEX

ACKNOWLEDGEMENTS

This book is unconventional in that even though it has taken me only a couple of years to write, I have been amassing the knowledge to be able to write it for a very long time. A lot of people have contributed to that, and it would be impossible to list all of them here. Having said that, on a recent trip to Valencia a bunch of magnificent chefs, who I can now call friends, helped me immensely by sharing their knowledge in the kitchen, on the rice fields, or in their *falla* (cultural collective). I am incredibly grateful for all the wisdom they imparted. Thank you for your hospitality and generosity César from L'olleta Club del Mar, Marcos from Arrocería Las Bairetas, Edu from Molino Roca, Juan from Arroz Tartana, Manuel from Casa Manolo, Alex from FoodVac, Segundo from Rincón del Varadero and Toni from Restaurante Elías. All restaurants that I highly recommend.

Special thanks to my dear amigo Dani who helped me begin writing this book and for your companionship on this journey. As usual, it's been so much fun.

At the forefront of my thoughts, thanks to my partner in crime Sandra, who is definitely the smartest of the two of us! You are our bright star and I look up to you. Thank you for taking the greatest care of our little Edu, Oscar and Noah. Thank you for being so genuinely supportive.

Thanks to my parents and mother-in-law, for being there for us unconditionally and helping us more than we could wish for. You make our lives so much greater and allow us a bit more freedom in the midst of these years of hard work and while building our young family. We are eternally grateful.

Thanks to my business partners who always support me and take care of the restaurants and our guests, and without whom everything would be that little bit harder.

Thanks to all the team at Quadrille: particularly Sarah, Harriet, Alicia, Clare, for believing in me and working so intelligently and hard on this book, which I couldn't be more proud of.

Thanks to Facundo (for whom this book has been his *ópera prima*), Lola, Rodo and all the team for the exquisite food and beautiful photography; you really captured the essence and vibe of paella!

And one last thank you to the people of Valencia, always willing, always helpful and always generous. Special thanks to Enrique Reyna and his loving family for welcoming us with open arms – and who are perfect examples of what is to be a Valenciano.

A NOTE FROM FACUNDO

To my dad looking from the sky, my mum, Mariano and Minos. Thank you for your love and support always, no matter what.

AUTHOR BIO

Madrid born, Omar Allibhoy is the founder of the critically acclaimed Tapas Revolution – a Spanish restaurant group in the UK. He began his career training under legendary chef Ferran Adrià then with Gordon Ramsay in London, who dubbed him the 'Antonio Banderas of cooking'. Since opening his first restaurant in 2010, he has been on a mission to showcase just how simple cooking Spanish cuisine at home can be. Omar is committed to being at the forefront of representing the wonderful food of Spain in the UK and has picked up multiple awards along the way. As well as running a successful business, Omar has maintained a career as a TV chef. He has two other books: *Tapas Revolution* and *Spanish Made Simple*.

MANAGING DIRECTOR Sarah Lavelle

COMMISSIONING EDITOR Harriet Webster

COPY EDITOR Clare Sayer

ART DIRECTION AND DESIGN Alicia House

PHOTOGRAPHER Facundo Bustamante

COVER ILLUSTRATION Melissa Donne

FOOD STYLISTS Lola Milne and Omar Allibhoy

PROP STYLIST Luis Peral

HEAD OF PRODUCTION Stephen Lang

SENIOR PRODUCTION CONTROLLER Sabeena Atchia

First published in 2023 by Quadrille Publishing Limited

Quadrille
52–54 Southwark Street
London SE1 1UN
quadrille.com

Reprinted in 2023, 2024 (twice)
10 9 8 7 6 5 4

ISBN: 978 1 78713 848 3

Printed in China